Enterprise
Architecture
as Strategy

Enterprise Architecture as Strategy

Creating a Foundation for
Business Execution

Jeanne W. Ross
Peter Weill
David C. Robertson

HARVARD BUSINESS SCHOOL PRESS
BOSTON, MASSACHUSETTS

978-1-59139-839-4 (ISBN 13)
Library of Congress Cataloging-in-Publication Data

Ross, Jeanne W.
Enterprise architecture as strategy : creating a foundation for business
execution / Jeanne W. Ross, Peter Weill, David C. Robertson.
p. cm.
Includes bibliographical references.
ISBN 1-59139-839-8
1. Industrial management—Automation. 2. Information technology—
Management. 3. Strategic planning. I. Weill, Peter. II. Robertson, David C.,
1935– III. Title.
HD45.2.R72 2006
658.4'038—dc22
2006010226

Contents

Preface and
Acknowledgments

In 1995 we started our study of enterprise architecture—we just didn't know it. At the time we thought we were studying information technology infrastructure transformations. In 1998 we thought we were studying enterprise system implementations. In 2000 it was e-business. But sometime in 2000, we recognized that each of these studies examined basically the same thing: enterprise architecture. We saw a pattern across those studies of what smart and profitable companies did differently. These companies made a commitment to a way of operating, and they were using IT to digitize that commitment. These companies kept getting better, faster, and more profitable at what they did while other companies were still figuring out what to do.

Most of the effort to define enterprise architecture has been located in companies' IT units. But the historic ineffectiveness of IT architecture efforts in large organizations has troubled us for years. In presentations we have railed against traditional IT architecture efforts for their remoteness from the reality of the business and their heavy reliance on mind-numbing detail represented in charts that look more like circuit diagrams than business descriptions and that are useful as little more than doorstops. All three of us have been frustrated by our inability in our research and executive education to make a breakthrough in understanding and improving IT architecture efforts. Until now . . .

It is now clear our problem was the level of analysis. As Albert Einstein famously remarked, "The significant problems we face cannot be solved by the same level of thinking that created them." The problem with our efforts to understand IT architecture was that the level of analysis was all wrong. The focus needs to be higher—on *enterprise architecture,* the organizing logic for core business processes and IT infrastructure reflecting the standardization and integration of a company's operating model. We have come to understand that enterprise architecture boils down to these two concepts: business process integration and business process standardization. In short, enterprise architecture is not an IT issue—it's a business issue.

The breakthrough in our understanding lay in an apparent contradiction. In a business world that is changing faster than ever before, the top-performing firms create a stable base—they digitize their core processes and embed those processes into a foundation for execution. This stable foundation makes a company both more efficient and more agile than its competitors. With global supply chains, pressure for ever faster time to market, more complex regulation, and huge shifts in customer demographics and desires, companies cannot predict the future. But they can decide what makes them great. And then they can create a low-cost, high-quality core of stability and constancy in a turbulent world. With a strong digitized core, great companies slide smoothly into the next opportunity while their competitors stumble.

Top-performing companies define how they will do business (an operating model) and design the processes and infrastructure critical to their current and future operations (enterprise architecture), which guide the evolution of their foundation for execution. Then these smart companies exploit their foundation, embedding new initiatives to make that foundation stronger, and using it as a competitive weapon to seize new business opportunities. And what makes this capability a competitive advantage is that only a small percentage of companies do it well—we estimate 5 percent of firms or less.

The objective of this book is to structure and explain what top-performing companies do so others can follow and improve. To inspire and illustrate what works well, we provide many examples of outstanding companies, including 7-Eleven Japan, CEMEX, Dow Chemical, ING DIRECT, MetLife, Schneider National, Toyota Motor Europe, UNICEF, UPS, and others. This book is about what makes a company great. Ultimately, of course, people make the difference. Good people design the operating model, build the foundation, execute, and innovate. But good people need direction, leadership, and incentives to perform at their best. This book is for managers, both business and IT, who sense the business problem and want to lead their organizations to build a solution—a unique digitized foundation for execution for their company.

The Research

The insights in the book come from a series of research projects exploring enterprise architecture in more than 200 companies (and another 256 companies where our focus was on IT governance) from 1995 to 2005. Most of the research was done at the MIT Sloan School's Center for Information Systems Research (CISR); the European work was done by David Robertson at IMD. The main studies were:

- Case studies of eighteen firms' implementations of new infrastructure capabilities, enterprise resource planning systems, and e-business initiatives by Jeanne Ross, Michael Vitale, and Peter Weill between 1995 and 2005. The cases focused on transformations leading to—and in some cases driven by—new IT capabilities. Companies included Australia Post, Brady Corp., Chase Manhattan, the District of Columbia's city government, Dow Corning, GTECH, JC Penney, Johnson & Johnson, Manheim Auctions, MetLife, Schneider National, Texas Instruments, Travelers, and five others.

- Case studies at eight companies on the relationship between IT and business strategy by Jeanne Ross and Peter Weill during 2001 and 2002. We studied how firms developed IT capabilities in response to business strategy. We also looked at how IT units were developing and managing enterprise architecture. Companies included Air Products and Chemicals, Citibank Asia Pacific, Delta Air Lines, DuPont, Merrill Lynch, Nestlé USA, Toyota USA, and UPS.

- Case studies on enterprise architecture at sixteen companies in the United States and Europe by David C. Robertson, Jeanne Ross, George Westerman, and Nils O. Fonstad in 2002. We studied how IT architecture enabled and constrained business initiatives. We also looked at how companies defined and managed business and technology standards. Cases were based on interviews with the CIO, IT architect, two project heads, and others at Akzo Nobel, BIC Graphic Europe, BT, Campbell Soup Co., Canon Europe, Carlson Companies, ING DIRECT, Marriott, Novartis, Panalpina, Partners HealthCare, Pfizer, Sécheron, Swisscom Mobile, Tetra Pak, and Toyota Motor Marketing Europe.

- Surveys of 103 firms to assess architecture outcomes by Jeanne Ross and Nils O. Fonstad in 2004. We examined IT investments, architecture management practices, architecture maturity, and IT and business outcomes.

- Surveys of eighty firms' IT and business process outsourcing initiatives by Jeanne Ross and Cynthia Beath in 2004 in conjunction with Lorraine Cosgrove at *CIO Magazine*. We examined the services outsourced, the characteristics of those services, the vendor-client relationship, architecture implications, and outcomes.

- Case studies of architectural implications of outsourcing at eight firms by Jeanne Ross, Cynthia Beath, Jeff Sampler, and Nils O. Fonstad during 2004 and 2005. We studied the role of enterprise architecture in outsourcing decisions and outcomes. The companies were Campbell Soup Co., Carlson Companies, Dow Chemical, eFunds, JM Family Enterprises, Tecnovate, and two others.

- Case studies by David C. Robertson and Nils O. Fonstad of Toyota Motor Marketing Europe, BT, ING DIRECT, and fifteen other companies to explore the key issues around establishing effective engagement models.

- In addition, we drew on a body of research on IT governance, including a study on effective IT governance led by Peter Weill with many colleagues from 2001 to 2004. We studied more than three hundred enterprises in twenty-three countries, including more than twenty-five in-depth case studies. We studied how enterprises made five key IT decisions, including architecture. We also measured governance and financial performance and what practices worked best.

Who Should Read this Book

This book is written for all executives who have ever wondered why some firms—and not others—achieve superior execution and are able to build on what they do well to achieve both agility and profitability. We describe the vision and steps to design an enterprise architecture and create a foundation for execution, highlighting the roles of both business and IT managers. We discuss the enterprise architecture decisions with enough detail to guide implementation. The language, style, data, examples, and lessons are about business issues that rely on technology.

We encourage senior managers, strategists, operational managers, marketing managers, financial managers, and IT managers to read this book and discuss building a foundation for execution in their companies. For simplicity of language we adopted the word *company* in this book. However, our comments relate equally to all organizations—whether they are large or small; for profit, not for profit, or government. Our intention is to capture the imagination and challenge the assumptions of managers in all industries as they build foundations for execution.

Whom We Would Like to Thank

We gratefully acknowledge the support of MIT CISR's patron and sponsor firms: Aetna, Allstate, American Express Company, AstraZeneca Pharmaceuticals LP, Biogen Idec, Inc., Boston Consulting Group, BT Group plc, Campbell Soup Co., CareFirst Blue Cross Blue Shield, CARE USA, Celanese, Chevron, Det Norske Veritas, DiamondCluster International, Direct Energy, eFunds Corporation, EMC Corporation, Gartner, Florida's Pasco County government, Guardian Life Insurance, Hewlett-Packard, ING Groep N.V., Intel Corporation, International Finance Corp., Merrill Lynch & Company, Inc., MetLife, Microsoft Corp., Mohegan Sun, Motorola, Inc., Nomura Research Institute, Ltd., PepsiAmericas, Inc, Pfizer, Inc., PFPC Inc., Raytheon Company, State Street Corp., Tata Consultancy Services–America, TD Banknorth, Telenor ASA, Trinity Health System, TRW Automotive, the U.N.'s Department of Economic and Social Affairs, and the U.S. Federal Aviation Administration. Executives from these enterprises not only inform and fund our research but also probe our assumptions, test our ideas, debate our findings, and implement and improve our work. We could not do this work without you.

During research and writing we have had the opportunity to work with many extraordinary managers and academic colleagues who have influenced our thinking and reinforced our passions. First, we would like to acknowledge the managers who shared their insights and, in many cases, provided the examples for the book. These managers included Toshifumi Suzuki, Makoto Usui, and Yuka Ozaki at 7-Eleven Japan; Al-Noor Ramji, Sinclair Stockman, Jan Cylwik, and Jim Crookes at BT; Doreen Wright at Campbell Soup Co.; Steve Brown, formerly of Carlson Companies; Karl Wachs at Celanese; John Bloom at Chevron; Frank Luijckx at Dow Chemical; Clyde Thomas and Kathleen Flanagan at eFunds; Dennis Callahan at Guardian Life Insurance; Martin Vonk and Rob Manders at ING DIRECT; Martin Curley and Malvina Nisman at Intel; Ken Yerves and Tom Holmes at JM Family Enterprises; David Henshaw and Phil Halsall at Liverpool Direct Ltd.; Jim McGrane at MeadWestvaco; Andy Brown at Merrill Lynch; Steve Sheinheit and Jerry Foster at MetLife; Chris Johnson at Nestlé; Monika Ribar at Panalpina; Ron Carter at Pfizer; Michael Harte at PFPC; Rebecca Rhoads, Kristine Ten Eck, Cassandra Matthews, and Alan G. Redfern at Raytheon; Brent Glendening at Schindler; Joe Antonellis, Ron Strout, and David Saul at State Street Corp.; John Petrey at TD Banknorth; Peter Heinckiens at Toyota Motor Marketing Europe; Andre Spatz at UNICEF; Mike Eskew, Ken Lacy, Jim Medeiros, and Dave Barnes at UPS.

We want to gratefully acknowledge all the managers who participated in case study interviews and those who took the time to answer our survey questions, add their own insights, and probe our assumptions. We are grateful to all of you for making this book possible.

Colleagues at other universities who contributed to the research in this book include Professor Cynthia M. Beath at the University of Texas at Austin, Professor Michael Vitale at the Australian Graduate School of Management, Professor Jeff Sampler at Oxford, and Professor Don Marchand at IMD.

We want to especially thank Drs. Nils O. Fonstad and George Westerman, research scientists at CISR, who participated in much of this research. Their contributions to this work were invaluable.

Thanks to Professor Ben Bensaou at INSEAD and Koki Yodokawa and Kei Nagayama at Nomura Research Institute in Japan who helped us understand why 7-Eleven Japan is so successful. Frank Erbrick at McKinsey & Co. and Charlie Feld at EDS enlightened us about enterprise architecture. We also want to thank the many people who provided important feedback on the research in this book, including Juan Ayala, Shafeen Charania, and Dinesh Kumar at Microsoft; Len Fehskens at HP; Con Kenney at the U.S. Federal Aviation Administration; Chuck Rieger at IBM; and Chris Curran and John Sviokla at DiamondCluster International. We'd also like to thank the members of the Advanced Practices Council of the Society for Information Management for their thoughtful feedback on this research. Thanks also to the many executives who made comments during our presentations or came up afterward to share their insights and critique.

In addition to three anonymous reviewers, three colleagues read the entire manuscript and provided not only valuable comments but also much appreciated enthusiasm and debate: Chris Curran at DiamondCluster, Dinesh Kumar at Microsoft, and Chuck Gibson at MIT CISR. Thank you for your input—you will see your comments reflected in this final version.

We also want to acknowledge Shafeen Charania of Microsoft for his insightful discussions and his strong advocacy of applying IT value research to enterprises around the world.

We wish to thank Lenny Zeltser, Charles Zedlewski, and Niraj Kumar, all researchers at MIT CISR who helped solicit companies and conduct interviews, and Mingdi Xin at New York University, who did detailed and painstaking quantitative analysis for this book. Individually and together as a team they added precision, professionalism, collegiality, and insight. We thank them.

Our MIT CISR colleague David Fitzgerald III managed the book production process with enthusiasm and professionalism. David devised the chapter template, produced the figures, enforced version control, tracked down citations, checked for contradictions, and almost kept us on schedule. We benefited from his experience and appreciated his dedication, flexibility, and especially his good humor.

The writing of this book, as well as our ongoing research efforts, would not be possible without the support of our other colleagues at MIT CISR and the MIT Sloan School of Management. Chris Foglia brings extraordinary talent and energy to the role of MIT CISR's center manager. She has proved that there is no technical, financial, artistic, or organizational issue at MIT CISR that she cannot address. Julie Coiro provides the friendly interface to MIT CISR. She has managed the organizational details that keep MIT CISR as a research center—and each of us as individuals—running smoothly. And we are indebted to our research colleagues George Westerman, Nils Fonstad (who co-authored chapter 6 of this book), Chuck Gibson, Jack Rockart, and Sinan Aral. We have benefited enormously from their insights, enthusiasm, hard work, and collegiality.

MIT CISR is a research center in the Sloan School of Management. We feel very fortunate to work in such a rich and exciting research environment. We have benefited, in particular, from the support and encouragement of Dean Richard Schmalensee, Dean Steven Eppinger, Professor Don Lessard, Professor Wanda Orlikowski, and Professor Tom Malone.

We would also like to thank Peter Lorange and Jim Ellert at IMD for the generous support IMD has provided for the European part of this research. Comparing experiences and testing our assumptions in a European context has deepened our understanding of the issues and broadened our thinking.

We are delighted to work with Kirsten Sandberg at Harvard Business School Press. Kirsten, as our editor on this and three previous books, knows just when to push and when to leave us to our own devices. Kirsten adds value in all the right places, and we thank her and her colleagues at HBS Press.

We undertook this book with a bit of trepidation as to the viability of writing as a trio. Getting three people to agree on ideas, text, figures, and organizing logic might have been exponentially tougher than two. Instead, we discovered that three heads are considerably better than one or two. Our different experiences, research styles, and perspectives led to interesting and valuable debates.

And the opportunity to work together was a joy. In writing this manuscript we found enormous satisfaction in the process of bringing together our different skills, challenging our assertions, and learning together. We are all more than ready to rededicate ourselves to our families, but we might even do this again.

A Personal Note from Jeanne

I'd first like to thank my family. I will remember this past summer fondly, not because of this book, but because our family of five adults had six precious weeks together. I reveled in our togetherness—five people loving one another, fixing meals, playing games, watching movies, telling stories, sharing joys, unloading frustrations, eating (constantly), teasing, laughing, and doing the little things that make us a family. It doesn't get any better. Thank you, Adam, for your curiosity and sensitivity; Julie, for your sense of adventure and fun; and Steffie, for your sweetness and joy. You are extraordinary blessings.

And to my husband, Dan, thank you for letting me be me. I appreciate all the sacrifices you made so that I could finish this manuscript. Thank you for your intensive reading of every chapter—you knew how to say "this doesn't make sense" in amazingly gentle and creative ways. This book is better for your contribution. And I am a better person for being married to you.

Finally, thank you to my parents, Mary and Russ Wenzel, and my in-laws, Jeanne and Irv Imburg—who offer their unwavering love and support, even as they wonder whether I'm taking on too much—and to my siblings, Pat and Jim, Jo, Barb and Mark, Russ and Diane, and Dave and Jill, who continue to teach me the joy of being family.

A Personal Note from Peter

The last year has been an amazing experience. In addition to having one of the greatest jobs in the world as director of MIT CISR and working on this book, I experienced a physical renewal. I went from not being able to walk without pain to regaining a normal life. I would like to thank Dr. Andrew Shimmin and his colleagues at the Melbourne Orthopaedic Group in Australia for giving me a new hip and a new lease on life. Thanks also to Tim Schleiger who made the rehab work both interesting and effective.

To my wife, Margi Olson, thank you for your understanding, support, love, and friendship. Without you this work would be meaningless. Somehow despite having your demanding day job as dean of Business and the Graduate School at Bentley College, you managed to be encouraging and delightful. Thank you for enthusiastically participating in endless dinner discussions on the difference between infrastructure and architecture and why some companies perform so well.

I hope the MBA students and executive education participants in my Sloan School courses recognize their input into this book. I thank them all as they contributed much in the way of learning, clarity, and focus during the countless discussions in session and out. I am constantly amazed and grateful about how much I learn from our interactions.

To my mother, Hidle Betty Weill. Thank you for your good genes, good humor, generous spirit, and most of all, love and support. To my brother Steve, as well as to Lois, David, and Simon—I love you guys. Together you complete my family in Australia and make my hometown so special. Finally, to my U.S.-based family, Geoffrey, Noa, and Ben Weill—thank you for making me feel part of a small but wonderful family Weill.

A Personal Note from David

First, a thank you to my colleagues at IMD who three years ago took a chance on a former enterprise software executive with no teaching experience. Many of you took extra time out of your busy schedules to help me learn the trade. IMD is a case study in how a high-performing organization can also be supportive and fun.

Thanks to Peter and Jeanne for keeping the wonderful institution of MIT CISR alive and thriving. MIT CISR has been, and continues to be, an island of sanity in the strange and wonderful world of MIT. Thank you both for letting me be part of such a great organization once again.

This work has benefited from many spirited discussions in IMD classrooms. Thanks especially to the participants from Credit Suisse, EMC, and Siemens for the many ideas you brought to this book. I look forward to continuing to work with you and learn from you.

To Phoebe, Alan, and Alice, thank you for all your love and support. To Gordon and Caroline, thank you for the constant joy you create. And to Anne, my foundation, thank you for your friendship, encouragement, and love.

1

To Execute Your Strategy, First Build Your Foundation

DOES IT FEEL AS IF the employees in your company are working harder and harder, but you're still losing ground? You've got great people, you invest carefully, and you believe you have the right strategy. You watch the market, listen to your customers, and react as quickly as you can to competitors' moves. In short, you do everything the management literature says you should, but you still can't get ahead.

And the signs aren't encouraging for the future. You see Chinese companies taking over manufacturing in industry after industry.[1] Indian companies providing more and more services.[2] Small, agile competitors from around the world picking off niche after niche in your markets. Competition is only getting tougher.

Yet some companies—some of your competitors—seem to be able not just to survive but to thrive. In the face of tough global competition, companies like Dell, ING DIRECT, CEMEX, Wal-Mart, and others are growing and making money. These companies have more-productive employees, get more from their investments, and have more success with their strategic initiatives. What are they doing differently?

We believe these companies execute better because they have a better foundation for execution. They have embedded technology in their processes so that they can efficiently and reliably execute the core operations of the company. These companies have made tough decisions about what operations they must execute well, and they've implemented the IT systems they need to digitize those operations. These actions have made IT an asset rather than a liability and have created a foundation for business agility.

We surveyed 103 U.S. and European companies about their IT and IT-enabled business processes. Thirty-four percent of those companies have digitized their core processes. Relative to their competitors, these companies have higher profitability, experience a faster time to market, and get more value from their IT investments.[3] They have better access to shared customer data, lower risk of mission-critical systems failures, and 80 percent higher senior management satisfaction with technology. Yet, companies who have digitized their core processes have 25 percent *lower* IT costs. These are the benefits of an effective foundation for execution.

In contrast, 12 percent of the companies we studied are frittering away management attention and technology investments on a myriad of (perhaps) locally sensible projects that don't support enterprisewide objectives. Another 48 percent of the companies are cutting waste from their IT budgets but haven't figured out how to increase value from IT. Meanwhile, a few leading-edge companies are leveraging a foundation for execution to pull further and further ahead.

As such statistics show, companies with a good foundation for execution have an increasing advantage over those that don't. In this book, we describe how to design, build, and leverage a foundation for execution. Based on survey and case study research at more than 400 companies in the United States and Europe, we provide insights, tools, and a language to help managers recognize their core operations, digitize their core to more efficiently support their strategy, and exploit their foundation for execution to achieve business agility and profitable growth.[4]

What Is a Foundation for Execution?

Every human being performs a variety of critical, fairly complex tasks without actually thinking about them. These tasks include breathing, hearing, swallowing, and seeing. With experience, humans can take on more-deliberate tasks like walking, riding a bike, driving a car, and making coffee. At first, these more-deliberate tasks require some concentration and adaptation, but they quickly become second nature. Over time, different humans develop distinguishing capabilities. A talented musician learns how to play piano; a great athlete plays basketball; a famous chef prepares extraordinary meals. Each of these distinctive capabilities has repeatable, routine activities that would be hard for a novice but that the expert can perform without thinking. Because experts need not focus on the routine activities in their field, they can concentrate on achieving greatness.

Companies are not blessed with the equivalent of the human brain, which coordinates all of a person's activities. Activities as simple as sending an invoice, taking an order, or mailing a package can easily go wrong—even after considerable practice. To focus management attention on higher-order processes, such as serving customers, responding to new business opportunities, and developing new products, managers need to limit the time they spend on what should be routine activities. They need to automate routine tasks so those tasks are performed reliably and predictably without requiring any thought.

A manufacturing company, for example, needs transparent information on customer orders, products shipped, finished goods inventory, raw materials inventory, work in process, invoices sent, payments received, and a host of related transaction data—just to perform at a minimally acceptable level. A mistake in any of that data can have ripple effects on a company's financial performance, its employee satisfaction, or its relationships with customers or suppliers. This is where a foundation for execution enters the picture. The foundation for execution digitizes these routine processes to provide reliability and predictability in processes that must go right. The best companies go beyond routine processes and digitize capabilities that distinguish them from their competitors.

For example, 7-Eleven Japan (SEJ) has built a foundation for execution that has helped make the convenience store chain the eighth-largest retailer in the world.[5] SEJ's foundation for execution allows each of the company's 10,000 stores to individually manage inventory while ensuring that they all generate rapid turnover on their large stocks of fresh foods. The underpinning for SEJ's foundation for execution is a network of 70,000 computers that collect data at the point of sale on every customer and every item sold. Each day the point-of-sale data is analyzed for use the next morning. Other digitized processes allow each store to place orders and receive deliveries three times each day. SEJ trains all of its 200,000 employees to use available point-of-sale, product, weather, and regional information not only to order from existing product lists but also to create hypotheses about possible new products. SEJ's foundation then connects employees with manufacturers to develop and test new items. The effect? In the average 7-Eleven store in Japan, 70 percent of the products sold each year are new.

In short, a *foundation for execution* is the IT infrastructure and digitized business processes automating a company's core capabilities. As with human development, a company's foundation for execution evolves—usually beginning with a few basic infrastructure services (e.g., employee hiring and recruiting, purchasing, desktop support, and telecommunications), then encompassing basic transaction processes (sales, accounts payable), and eventually including unique and distinguishing business capabilities. Building a foundation doesn't focus only on competitively distinctive capabilities—it also requires rationalizing and digitizing the mundane, everyday processes that a company has to get right to stay in business.[6]

Paradoxically, digitizing core business processes makes the individual processes less flexible while making a company more agile. To return to the human analogy, a great athlete will have muscles, reflexes, and skills that are not easily changed. But these capabilities give athletes a tremendous ability to react, improvise, and innovate in their chosen sport.[7] Similarly, digitizing business processes requires making clear decisions about what capabilities are needed to succeed. And once these new processes are installed, they free up management attention from fighting fires on lower-value activities, giving them more time to focus on how to increase profits and growth. Digitized processes also provide better information on customers and product sales, providing ideas for new products and services. The foundation for execution provides a platform for innovation.

Do You Have a Good Foundation for Execution?

In our visits to dozens of companies, we have learned to recognize the warning signs of a company that doesn't have a foundation that supports its strategy. Comments from senior executives like the following are indicators:

- Different parts of our company give different answers to the same customer questions.

- Meeting a new regulatory or reporting requirement is a major effort for us, requiring a concerted push from the top and significant infrastructure investment.

- Our business lacks agility—every new strategic initiative is like starting from scratch.

- IT is consistently a bottleneck.

- There are different business processes completing the same activity across the company, each with a different system.

- Information needed to make key product and customer decisions is not available.

- A significant part of people's jobs is to take data from one set of systems, manipulate it, and enter it into other systems.

- Senior management dreads discussing IT agenda items.

- We don't know whether our company gets good value from IT.

As those comments suggest, companies without an effective foundation for execution face serious competitive and regulatory threats.

An effective foundation for execution depends on tight alignment between business objectives and IT capabilities. Toward that end, most companies put in business processes and IT systems using a fairly straightforward logic. First, management defines a strategic direction; then the IT unit, ideally in conjunction with business management, designs a set of IT-enabled solutions to support the initiative; and, finally, the IT unit delivers the applications, data, and technology infrastructure to implement the solutions. The process starts over each time management defines another strategic initiative.

This process goes wrong in at least three ways. First, the strategy isn't always clear enough to act upon. General statements about the importance of "leveraging synergies" or "getting close to the customer" are difficult to implement. So the company builds IT solutions rather than IT capabilities. Second, even if the strategy is clear enough to act upon, the company implements it in a piecemeal, sequential process. Each strategic initiative results in a separate IT solution, each implemented on a different technology. Third, because IT is always reacting to the latest strategic initiative, IT is always a bottleneck. IT never becomes an asset shaping future strategic opportunities.

Figure 1-1 shows the combined effect of traditional approaches to IT development—a set of silos. Individually, the applications work fine. Together, they hinder companies' efforts to coordinate customer, supplier, and employee processes—they do not form a foundation for execution. And the company's data, one of its most important assets, is patchy, error-prone, and not up to date. Companies often extract from silos to aggregate data from multiple systems in a data warehouse (the cloud in figure 1-1). But the warehouse is useful only as a reference—it does not offer real-time data across applications.

The many squiggly lines in figure 1-1 reflect efforts to integrate isolated systems supporting an end-to-end process. One IT executive in an investment banking company claimed that 80 percent of his company's programming code was dedicated to linking disparate systems, as opposed to creating new capabilities. This executive bragged that his developers were able to link together systems so effectively that no human being ever touched a transaction—every process was supported end-to-end by meticulously

FIGURE 1-1

Capability from traditional approach to IT solutions

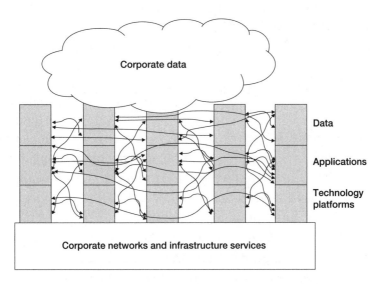

© 2005 MIT Sloan Center for Information Systems Research and IMD. Used with permission.

integrated silo applications. But then he noted, "It's a miracle they work." Eventually this company's lack of a foundation for execution made it a juicy takeover target. Today these systems are being replaced with those of the acquiring company.

Few companies are comfortable with a dependency on miracles. They want technology to reliably support existing processes. What's more, they'd like their existing technology to enable future capabilities. These companies need to take a different approach to implementing IT-enabled business processes.

How Do You Build a Foundation for Execution?

The foundation for execution results from carefully selecting which processes and IT systems to standardize and integrate. Just as humans must learn how to ride a bicycle (and think hard about what they are doing while they are learning), the processes built into a foundation for execution require a great deal of concentration—for a while. Eventually routine business activities—just like bicycle riding—become automatic. Outcomes become predictable. The foundation for execution takes on another layer. A company's identity becomes clearer, and executives can focus their attention on the future.

To build an effective foundation for execution, companies must master three key disciplines:

1. *Operating model.* The *operating model* is the necessary level of business process integration and standardization for delivering goods and services to customers. Different companies have different levels of process integration across their business units (i.e., the extent to which business units share data). Integration enables end-to-end processing and a single face to the customer, but it forces a common understanding of data across diverse business units. Thus, companies need to make overt decisions about the

importance of process integration. Management also must decide on the appropriate level of business process standardization (i.e., the extent to which business units will perform the same processes the same way). Process standardization creates efficiencies across business units but limits opportunities to customize services. The operating model involves a commitment to how the company will operate.

2. *Enterprise architecture.* The *enterprise architecture* is the organizing logic for business processes and IT infrastructure, reflecting the integration and standardization requirements of the company's operating model. The enterprise architecture provides a long-term view of a company's processes, systems, and technologies so that individual projects can build capabilities—not just fulfill immediate needs. Companies go through four stages in learning how to take an enterprise architecture approach to designing business processes: Business Silos, Standardized Technology, Optimized Core, and Business Modularity. As a company advances through the stages, its foundation for execution takes on increased strategic importance.

3. *IT engagement model.* The *IT engagement model* is the system of governance mechanisms that ensure business and IT projects achieve both local and companywide objectives. The IT engagement model influences project decisions so that individual solutions are guided by the enterprise architecture. The engagement model provides for alignment between the IT and business objectives of projects, and coordinates the IT and business process decisions made at multiple organizational levels (e.g., companywide, business unit, project). To do so, the model establishes linkages between senior-level IT decisions, such as project prioritization and companywide process design, and project-level implementation decisions.

FIGURE 1-2

Creating and exploiting the foundation for execution

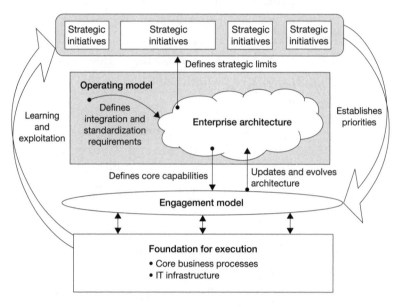

© 2005 MIT Sloan Center for Information Systems Research and IMD. Used with permission.

Figure 1-2 illustrates how companies apply these three disciplines to create and exploit their foundation for execution. Based on the vision of how the company will operate (the operating model), business and IT leaders define key architectural requirements of the foundation for execution (the enterprise architecture). Then, as business leaders identify business initiatives, the IT engagement model specifies how each project benefits from, and contributes to, the foundation for execution.

Why Is a Foundation for Execution Important?

Our research found that companies with a solid foundation had higher profitability, faster time to market, and lower IT costs. These outcomes are universally beneficial and timeless—they were valuable twenty years ago and will be just as valuable twenty years from now. But there are a number of more-recent developments that highlight the increasing importance of a foundation for execution. Companies without a solid foundation face a number of serious risks that weren't present just ten years ago.

Growing Complexity in Companies' Systems Can Fossilize Operations

As with the investment bank whose systems were so complex that it was a miracle they worked, legacy systems cobbled together to respond to each new business initiative create rigidity and excessive costs. The Internet boom exposed the inflexibility of many companies' technology and process environments, which led to an inability to adapt to new channels. This inflexibility was not the result of a digitized foundation for execution. It was the result of systems so complex that any change required individually rewiring systems to all the other systems they connect to. Developing and testing new capabilities in such a complex environment is time consuming, and every change becomes a risky, expensive adventure.

The complexity has not added value. Most managers can list processes they perform in many different ways in multiple parts of the company and support with many different systems. As more competitors aggressively pursue reuse of standard processes and systems across their product lines, services, or business units, the inefficiencies of non-value-added variations create strategic disadvantages. The CIO at a $5 billion manufacturing company reported that a global implementation of three modules of a large, packaged enterprise resource planning system (make to ship, account to report, and order to cash) eliminated 450 applications and 3,150 interfaces, mostly by eliminating redundancy. Implementing standardized, digitized processes carries costs, particularly those associated with organizational change, but the benefits are simpler technology environments, lower-cost operations, and greater agility.[8]

Business Agility Increasingly Depends on a Foundation for Execution

Business agility is becoming a strategic necessity. Greater global-ization, increasing regulation, and faster cycle times all demand an ability to quickly change organizational processes. Managers can-not predict what will change, but they can predict some things that won't change. And if they digitize what is not changing, they can focus on what is changing. In this way the foundation for ex-ecution becomes a foundation for agility.

There are many types of agility, but one indicator of agility is a company's percentage of revenue generated from new products. Our research on 147 companies found that, from 1998 to 2002, on average, 24 percent of a company's sales were from new products introduced in the prior three years. But this percentage varied greatly from company to company—even between those in the same industry. For example, in manufacturing the average was 24 percent. However, a third of companies achieved 50 percent of sales from new products introduced in the prior three years.[9] These more-agile companies also had a high percentage of their core business processes digitized. While there are many possible explanations for differences in a single type of agility, having a digitized foundation for execution probably enabled managers in these companies to spend more time focusing on what products would succeed and then bringing those products to market.

Current National and Political Environments Demand Business Discipline

Companies are buffeted by constant changes in regulations, such as Sarbanes-Oxley, Basel II, and HIPAA.[10] As companies become more global, they become accountable for increasingly complex reporting requirements. And some industries, particularly health care and financial services, face different laws and regulations in different regions of the same country.

For many companies, new regulations mean massive expenditures with no added value. But companies with a solid foundation for execution have more transparent information and the ability to access data more quickly. For example, a financial services company executive commented that Sarbanes-Oxley had not involved any system changes in his company; the required data was already available due to processes the company had implemented. Companies may not be able to anticipate new regulations, but they can increase the likelihood that needed data is readily available or can easily be accumulated.

Building a Foundation Is Less Risky and Expensive Than the Alternative

Many managers, scarred by their experiences in the late 1990s with enterprise resource planning system implementations, think that implementing improvements is going to be an expensive, risky proposition.[11] However, as we will describe in chapter 6, most companies don't have to make massive investments in their foundation. The foundation for execution can be implemented one project at a time. By spending smarter rather than more, companies can use ongoing projects to steadily build their foundation for execution. And as the foundation gets built, IT costs decrease and business efficiencies increase, paying dividends on the original investment.

How Does a Foundation for Execution Create Business Value?

To illustrate the concept of a foundation for execution and its potential impact on a company, we provide two brief case studies. The first is on UPS, a company well known for its use of IT in business processes. UPS has been building and leveraging its foundation for execution since the late 1980s.

UPS: Building New Services on a Solid Foundation

Around 1986 senior management at UPS became concerned about the company's inability to respond to competitors' technology-based market initiatives. UPS had dominated the U.S. package delivery market for much of its eighty years, but management recognized that the company would need a strong IT capability to compete in the future. Over the next ten years, UPS built a foundation for execution that has permitted it to seize global market opportunities not only in package delivery but also in a variety of related areas.

Although its immediate concern was package tracking (i.e., reporting on the whereabouts of a package in transit), UPS set out to build a foundation for execution embodying its industrial-engineering tradition (figure 1-3). The company has long employed a large staff of industrial engineers who study efficiency and design optimal business processes. Industrial engineers have specified efficient processes for a wide range of tasks at UPS, including which foot a driver should put into the truck first. The company implements these processes as global standards. Thus, when the company was debating the requirements of an IT capability, it was clear to all key decision makers that systems would have to support UPS's global process standards. In addition, management agreed that the nature of package delivery demanded highly integrated systems, so that a package could not be lost en route.

UPS's new CIO and his staff developed an enterprise architecture to reflect the company's goals. A key characteristic of the enterprise architecture was the specification for a single package database. The CIO did not want multiple package databases, which would risk the integrity of the data. The CIO's team also emphasized the need for a global telecommunications capability so that the package data could be captured and accessed from anywhere a package might be picked up or delivered. The company developed strict rules about architectural standards, and IT was authorized to enforce the rules whenever a breach could compromise reliability or efficiency.

FIGURE 1-3

UPS's foundation for execution

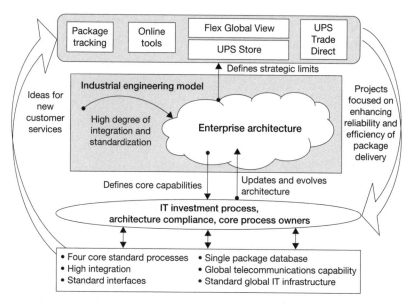

Source: Researcher interpretation.

© 2005 MIT Sloan Center for Information Systems Research and IMD. Used with permission.

On the business process side, senior management defined four core processes: package delivery, product development, customer relationship management, and customer information management. UPS standardized tasks within these processes as appropriate so that new initiatives could leverage existing capabilities. Starting from package tracking and related core processes, UPS leveraged its systems and process capabilities first by adding channels, such as the Internet. Then UPS expanded into new services. For example, Flex Global View allowed customers to receive advance notification of incoming packages and to track packages traveling with freight forwarders or other UPS partners. Flex Global View also notified customers if any packages would arrive late. Building on these capabilities, UPS grew from a package delivery company into a global commerce company. UPS Trade Direct, one of the company's newer offerings, provides integrated door-to-door service for international packages, including consolidated billing, customs brokerage and clearance, and international package tracking.

UPS's innovations build on or leverage its existing foundation for execution and create new opportunities. Because of the strategic importance of IT at UPS, IT leaders are consistently involved in strategy discussions and propose new products and services based on existing capabilities. Regarding the IT unit's input to strategy discussions, Mike Eskew, UPS's CEO comments, "I get that kind of happy surprise from IT all the time."[12] Happy surprises from IT—that's what a foundation for execution has done for UPS.

Washington, D.C.: Customer-Focused Service Delivery

Throughout the book we mostly refer to the needs of companies. But the principles of the foundation for execution are equally relevant for public and private companies, government agencies, and not-for-profit organizations. Performance objectives and some metrics may differ by type of organization, but the need to enable efficient, reliable, agile operations is the same. The government of the District of Columbia has been building a foundation for execution since 1999. Organizations of all kinds might find its experience instructive.

Excluding its public school system, Washington, D.C., has 21,000 employees and a $5.4 billion budget, managed by an appointed city administrator who is accountable to the mayor and the D.C. council. Services are provided through seventy-four operating agencies, ten of which provide centralized administrative services (e.g., purchasing, human resources, information technology, legal services), and sixty-four of which provide customer-facing services (e.g., law enforcement, children's services, transportation). When Anthony Williams was inaugurated as mayor in January

1999, the District of Columbia was half a billion dollars in debt. Its public services were ranked at the bottom of big-city service ratings, and control of the district's administration was in the hands of a federally appointed board. Citizens complained of poor service: the process of registering a car could take a full day, and small-business owners often hired experts to represent them in the maze of offices at the Department of Consumer and Regulatory Affairs.

Mayor Williams committed to turning the district around and improving services to the city's residents and visitors. The CTO, Suzanne Peck, recognized that as a public service—as opposed to a business—the district's customers had no choice about interacting with its agencies. If residents wanted a license, or dog tags, or to pay their taxes, they had to deal with the government agencies. The Williams administration's goal was to make these interactions as pleasant and efficient as possible. Consequently, the CTO adopted the following set of operating tenets for interactions with constituents:

- *A single point of entry.* All citizen requests must be routed to a central point of entry so that citizens are not left to wander helplessly among seventy-four agencies to find what they need.

- *Guaranteed closure.* All citizens must be assured that their requests, once submitted, will be fulfilled, no matter which agency or how many agencies are involved in the transaction.

- *Benign service delivery.* Residents have no choice but to deal with government, so the CTO's office will make dealing with the government as positive as possible. Peck emphasized the goal of benign service delivery: "As a District, the finest thing I can do for you, the residents, is to give you benign service delivery. I can make it easy for you to deal with me. I can make it not horrible."[13]

The district's operating model—including its concept of benign service delivery—called for standardization of common processes. The operating model also provided for end-to-end integration of processes, as well as data sharing, between related agencies (figure 1-4). At the heart of the district's enterprise architecture are nine service modernization programs, which represent functional clusters of the district's multiagency systems. Each of the district's 370 systems fits functionally into one of those nine programs: administrative, customer, educational, enforcement, financial, human, motorist, property, and transportation services. The service programs create standard, multiagency, end-to-end processes for the district.

FIGURE 1-4

D.C. government's foundation for execution

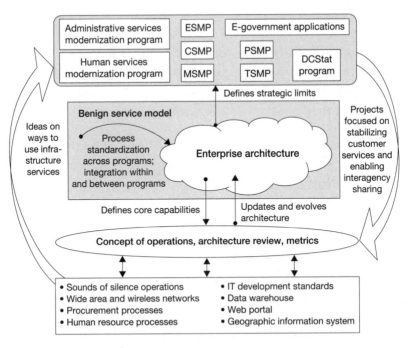

Source: Researcher interpretation.

© 2005 MIT Sloan Center for Information Systems Research and IMD. Used with permission.

Before beginning any major application process improvements, Peck focused on first stabilizing operations and developing some core infrastructure services, including WAN and wireless services; the consolidation of servers, storage, and software; and the introduction of disciplined management practices such as development standards. The new infrastructure services introduced cost savings and new capabilities. For example, the cost of telephony services decreased by 33 percent while capacity increased by a factor of 1,600.

The first major application improvement project was the administrative services program. Although administrative services was not customer facing, the agencies that were customer facing reported that poor administrative services—such as snafus in hiring, lost grant applications, and purchasing difficulties—were severely hindering their ability to service customers. As with all improvements, the first step was to define a concept of operations that described the desired customer experience with the service.

The administrative services modernization program kicked off in 2001 as a five-year $71 million program with measurable cost savings of $150 million. An architecture review board reviewed each concept of operations for architectural compliance and continued to monitor the architecture throughout the implementation of each new process. In the third year of the program, management had already documented $50 million in annual cost savings due to improved procurement, recruiting and hiring, and related services.

The district has been initiating new projects incrementally, building on its experiences with prior projects, and reusing infrastructure introduced for one project in subsequent projects. For example, the office of the CTO is building a portal that has become a key interface as new services are introduced. The D.C. government's Web site grew from twenty pages in 1999 to almost 200,000 in 2005. The Web site transformed from a public embarrassment to one that *Government Technology* magazine named the number one Web portal in government. More important, in just a few years, the D.C. government has gone, in the words of Suzanne Peck, "from worst to first."

Goals and Overview of the Book

UPS's experience with happy surprises from IT and its ability to design new products and services that leverage its foundation for execution is exceptional relative to most companies we've studied. But, like the District of Columbia government, companies are increasingly experiencing incremental, but significant, operating improvements as they build and leverage a foundation for execution. Building a foundation is not a quick or easy process. This book is a call to action for those companies that have not yet started on this journey and a handbook for those who are in the midst of building their foundation. In this book we describe how to (1) define an operating model, (2) design and implement an enterprise architecture, and (3) adopt an IT engagement model. In doing so, we describe how your company can achieve greatness with a foundation for execution.

Companies that build a solid foundation for execution do achieve greatness. Throughout this book we will describe the IT and business process capabilities of companies generating strategic benefits from their foundations. These companies include the following:

- *ING DIRECT:* the number one direct bank (in terms of retail funds entrusted) in every one of the nine countries in which it operates. ING DIRECT's operational costs are only 0.43 percent of assets, as compared to 2.5 percent for a typical full-service bank, allowing the company to offer higher savings rates and lower-cost loans than other banks. The result has been phenomenal growth. In the first quarter of 2005, ING DIRECT grew an average of 250,000 new customers and more than $5 billion in new assets each month.

- *7-Eleven Japan:* the most profitable retailer in Japan and the eighth-largest retailer in the world. Since its inception as a single store in 1973, 7-Eleven Japan has grown to

10,800 stores in Japan. Worldwide 7-Eleven Japan has 28,000 stores and annual revenues of ¥25,000 billion (approx US$22 billion). Gross margins per store have increased from 5 percent to more than 30 percent from 1977 to 2004. Management has reduced stock turnover from 25.5 days in 1977 to fewer than 8.7 days in 2004.[14]

- *TD Banknorth: Forbes's* "best managed" bank for 2004, due to the company's steady earnings growth of 10 percent or more. TD Banknorth has acquired twenty-six banks in the past eleven years, and since 1989, it has grown from $2 billion to $32 billion. TD Banknorth is second among banks in the *Fortune* 1000 in total return to shareholders (a 37% annual rate from 1991 to 2001).[15]

This book is intended for senior managers who have—or believe they should take—responsibility for developing and overseeing their company's foundation for execution. Business executives should finish this book with a clear understanding of what they need to do to lead the change and engage their business and IT colleagues in discussions on how to create a foundation for execution. IT executives should finish this book with a clear frame of reference for their work and the tools to successfully work with their business colleagues. Building a foundation for execution requires extraordinary IT-business alignment, so both IT and business leaders need to exert influence on the process. The result is worth the trouble.

The structure of the book is as follows:

- *Chapter 2: Define Your Operating Model.* In chapter 2 we introduce the first discipline for creating the foundation for execution: the operating model and its two key dimensions—business process standardization and integration. Four different types of operating models are described: Unification, Coordination, Replication, and Diversification. We explore how the operating model concept is applied to both companies and business units. Case studies of JM Family Enterprises, Merrill Lynch, Dow Chemical, TD Banknorth, and Schneider National provide examples of different operating models.

- *Chapter 3: Implement the Operating Model Via Enterprise Architecture.* In chapter 3 we introduce the second discipline for creating the foundation for execution: the enterprise architecture. The key elements—digitized business processes, IT infrastructure, shared data, and customer interfaces—are identified and linked in the enterprise architecture. The one-page core diagram is introduced, and comparative diagrams are developed for each of the four operating models. Four case studies of firms and their enterprise architecture designs illustrate effective practices: MetLife, ING DIRECT, Carlson Companies, and Delta Air Lines.

- *Chapter 4: Navigate the Stages of Enterprise Architecture Maturity.* In chapter 4 we introduce the four stages of enterprise architecture maturity: Business Silos, Standardized Technology, Optimized Core, and Business Modularity. Companies traverse these stages as they learn new organizational processes and change their IT investment practices. We describe how the strategic value of IT evolves as companies mature their enterprise architectures. A number of short examples illustrate the concepts, and we conclude with a discussion of how to apply the architecture stages in your company.

- *Chapter 5: Cash In on the Learning.* In chapter 5 we explain how companies get unique business benefits at each of the four stages of maturity by using various management practices and roles. We explain how achieving these benefits requires implementing different management mechanisms at each stage to formalize organizational learning. A case study of Schindler illustrates how the role of the CIO evolves as companies move through the maturity stages.

- *Chapter 6: Build the Foundation One Project at a Time.* In chapter 6 we introduce the third discipline for creating the foundation for execution: the IT engagement model. The IT engagement model has three ingredients: IT governance, project management, and linkages connecting the two. A good engagement model enables a company to build its foundation one project at a time. Case studies of Raytheon and Toyota Motor Marketing Europe illustrate the different ingredients of the model.

- *Chapter 7: Use Enterprise Architecture to Guide Outsourcing.* In chapter 7 we describe how outsourcing can contribute to enterprise architecture maturity but warn that outsourcing success is far from guaranteed. To improve the likelihood of success, we show how to use the operating model and enterprise architecture to determine what and when to outsource. We distinguish between three different types of outsourcing—strategic partnerships, cosourcing alliances, and transaction relationships. Analyzing the experiences of Campbell Soup Co. and the City of Liverpool, we discuss how outsourcing can affect enterprise architecture, and vice versa. A case study illustrates how Dow Chemical aggressively uses outsourcing—driven by its enterprise architecture—to move to what it calls the "Federated Broker Model."

- *Chapter 8: Now—Exploit Your Foundation for Profitable Growth.* In chapter 8 we make the urgent case for increased agility in companies that must compete in a global economy. Case studies of UPS, 7-Eleven Japan, and MetLife illustrate the growth potential of different operating models. A case study of CEMEX highlights the architectural challenges created by acquisitions. We close the chapter with a look at what's coming next—the fifth stage of architecture maturity.

- *Chapter 9: Take Charge! The Leadership Agenda.* Chapter 9 summarizes the key ideas in the book with a review of the symptoms of an ineffective foundation for execution. We follow with a set of six steps for rethinking your foundation for execution. Then we provide ten leadership principles for building and leveraging a foundation for execution.

2

Define Your Operating Model

GENERAL H. NORMAN SCHWARZKOPF once observed, "Leadership is a potent combination of strategy and character. But if you must be without one, be without the strategy."[1] Few business executives would be comfortable leading without a strategy. Business strategy provides direction, an impetus for action. Most companies also rely on strategy to guide IT investments. Accordingly, IT executives work to align IT and IT-enabled business processes with stated business strategy. But business-IT strategic alignment can be an elusive goal.

Business strategies are multifaceted, encompassing decisions as to which markets to compete in, how to position the company in each market, and which capabilities to develop and leverage. In addition, strategic priorities can shift as companies attempt to respond to competitor initiatives or to seize new opportunities. As a result, strategy rarely offers clear direction for development of stable IT infrastructure and business process capabilities.

To best support a company's strategy, we recommend that the company define an operating model. An *operating model* is the necessary level of business process integration and standardization for delivering goods and services to customers. An operating model describes how a company wants to thrive and grow. By providing a more stable and actionable view of the company than strategy, the operating model drives the design of the foundation for execution.

The choice of an operating model is a critical decision for a company. It's the first step in building a foundation for execution. An operating model enables rapid implementation of a range of strategic initiatives. But that same operating model will fail to support initiatives that are inconsistent with the assumptions it's built on. Thus, the operating model is a choice about what strategies are going to be supported. Take, for example, the ease with which Charles Schwab introduced online brokerage relative to Morgan Stanley. Schwab had already implemented low-touch systems and processes. In contrast, Morgan Stanley had built its capabilities for more customer-intimate (and higher-cost) operations. Similarly, Amazon could add consumer products to its product list because its operating model highlighted its capabilities in distribution and online customer interactions. Barnes & Noble's operating model was ill-suited to online sales but adapted easily to a partnership with Starbucks, which enhanced its customers' in-store shopping experience.

The operating model decision (or lack thereof) has a profound impact on how a company implements business processes and IT infrastructure. A company without a clear operating model brings no automated, preexisting, low-cost capabilities to a new strategic pursuit. Instead, with each new strategic initiative the company must effectively begin anew to identify its key capabilities. But selecting an operating model is a commitment to a way of doing business. That can be a daunting choice.

Our research suggests the payoff for making that choice can be huge. Companies with a foundation for execution supporting an operating model reported 17 percent greater strategic effectiveness than other companies—a metric positively correlated with profitability.[2] These companies also reported higher operational efficiency (31%), customer intimacy (33%), product leadership (34%), and strategic agility (29%) than companies that had not developed a foundation for execution.[3]

In this chapter we will first define the dimensions of the operating model—standardization and integration—and then describe the four types of operating models: Diversification, Coordination, Unification, and Replication. We will describe the critical components of each model and show how an operating model shapes future strategic choices. We will then discuss important considerations in choosing an operating model.

Integration and Standardization: Key Dimensions of an Operating Model

An operating model has two dimensions: business process standardization and integration. Although we often think of standardization and integration as two sides of the same coin, they impose different demands. Executives need to recognize standardization and integration as two separate decisions.

Standardization of business processes and related systems means defining exactly how a process will be executed regardless of who is performing the process or where it is completed. Process standardization delivers efficiency and predictability across the company. For example, using a standard process for selling products or buying supplies allows the activities of different business units to be measured, compared, and improved. The result of standardization—a reduction in variability—can be dramatic increases in throughput and efficiency.

Yet greater standardization has a cost. In exchange for increased predictability, standardized processes necessarily limit local innovation. And the transition to standardization usually requires that perfectly good (and occasionally superior) systems and processes be ripped out and replaced by the new standard. This can be politically difficult and expensive.

Integration links the efforts of organizational units through shared data. This sharing of data can be between processes to enable end-to-end transaction processing, or across processes to allow the company to present a single face to customers. For example, an automobile manufacturer may decide to integrate processes so that when a sale is recorded, the car is reserved from among the cars currently in production. By seamlessly sharing data between the order management and manufacturing scheduling processes, the company improves its internal integration and, consequently, its customer service. In financial services, sharing data across processes enables a loan officer to review a customer's checking, savings, and brokerage accounts with the bank, providing better information about the customer's financial situation and enabling better risk assessments for loans.

The benefits of integration include increased efficiency, coordination, transparency, and agility. An integrated set of business processes can improve customer service, provide management with better information to make decisions, and allow changes in one part of the business to alert other parts of actions they need to take. Integration can also speed up the overall flow of information and transactions through a company.

The biggest challenge of integration is usually around data. End-to-end integration requires companies to develop standard definitions and formats for data that will be shared across business units or functions. For business units to share customer information, they must agree on its format. Similarly, they must share a common definition for terms like *sale,* which can be said to occur when a contract is signed, when money is paid, or when product is delivered. These can be difficult, time-consuming decisions.

Four Types of Operating Models

We have developed a straightforward two-dimensional model with four quadrants, representing different combinations of the levels of business process integration and standardization (figure 2-1). Every company should position itself in one of these quadrants to clarify how it intends to deliver goods and services to customers.

The four general types of operating models are:

1. Diversification (low standardization, low integration)

2. Coordination (low standardization, high integration)

3. Replication (high standardization, low integration)

4. Unification (high standardization, high integration)

FIGURE 2-1

Characteristics of four operating models

Coordination	Unification
• Shared customers, products, or suppliers • Impact on other business unit transactions • Operationally unique business units or functions • Autonomous business management • Business unit control over business process design • Shared customer/supplier/product data • Consensus processes for designing IT infrastructure services; IT application decisions made in business units	• Customers and suppliers may be local or global • Globally integrated business processes often with support of enterprise systems • Business units with similar or overlapping operations • Centralized management often applying functional/process/business unit matrices • High-level process owners design standardized processes • Centrally mandated databases • IT decisions made centrally
Diversification	**Replication**
• Few, if any, shared customers or suppliers • Independent transactions • Operationally unique business units • Autonomous business management • Business unit control over business process design • Few data standards across business units • Most IT decisions made within business units	• Few, if any, shared customers • Independent transactions aggregated at a high level • Operationally similar business units • Autonomous business unit leaders with limited discretion over processes • Centralized (or federal) control over business process design • Standardized data definitions but data locally owned with some aggregation at corporate • Centrally mandated IT services

Business process integration — High / Low

Low   High

Business process standardization

Companies adopt an operating model at the enterprise level and may adopt different operating models at the division, business unit, region, or other level. To decide which quadrant your company (or business unit) belongs in, ask yourself two questions:

1. To what extent is the successful completion of one business unit's transactions dependent on the availability, accuracy, and timeliness of other business units' data?

2. To what extent does the company benefit by having business units run their operations in the same way?

The first question determines your integration requirements; the second, your standardization requirements. What operating model you choose will drive important design decisions around the autonomy of business unit managers and the role of IT. Compare your answers to the characteristics of each operating model in figure 2-1 to see where your company fits.

Diversification: Independence with Shared Services

Diversification applies to companies whose business units have few common customers, suppliers, or ways of doing business. Business units in diversified companies offer different products and services to different customers, so central management exercises limited control over those business units (see the Diversification quadrant in figure 2-1).

JM Family Enterprises (JMFE) has a Diversification operating model. Headquartered in Deerfield Beach, Florida, JMFE had revenues of $8.2 billion in 2004, making it the United States' fifteenth-largest privately held company.[4] JMFE comprises four closely related businesses:

1. Southeast Toyota Distributors (SET) serves more than 160 dealers in Florida, Georgia, Alabama, and North and South Carolina with vehicles, parts, and accessories. SET dealers sell approximately 20 percent of all Toyotas sold in the United States.

2. World Omni Financial Corp. (WOFC) is a diversified financial services company that provides a broad range of financial products and services to consumers, dealers, and lenders. Its offerings include automotive financial products and services, third-party servicing solutions, wholesale floor-plan accounting and risk management systems, full-service inspection, automated risk decision software, and automotive remarketing services.

3. JM&A Group offers a variety of automotive finance and insurance (F&I) products and services, such as new- and used-vehicle protection plans, used-vehicle certification programs, prepaid maintenance plans, credit life and disability insurance, and F&I training and consulting services.

4. JM Lexus is the largest-volume retail dealership of Lexus cars and sport-utility vehicles in the world.

The lower left quadrant of figure 2-2 describes JMFE's Diversification operating model. Because the business units are synergistic, they can generate business for one another. For example, JM Lexus is a customer of JM&A; SET sells automobiles to dealers whose customers often finance those vehicles through WOFC; and WOFC offers loans to dealers to finance the vehicles in stock, helping increase orders to SET.

JMFE provides some centralized services to its business units through the JM Service Center. The largest of the shared services is IT; the others are procurement services, financial services, salon, fitness center, benefits administration, food services, corporate staffing, distributive and document services, facilities, relocation, and dealer services. Motivation for forming shared services in 2001 included cutting costs on these services and realizing quick economies following expected acquisitions.

Historically, JMFE has grown primarily through the growth of individual business units. SET has become the world's largest franchised Toyota distributor, and WOFC is one of the world's largest automotive finance companies. As JMFE's current markets become

FIGURE 2-2

Four operating model examples

Coordination	**Unification**
Merrill Lynch Global Private Client	**Dow Chemical**
• Single face to customer through multiple channels	• Local and global customers; global suppliers
• Customer transactions are independent, but product data is shared	• Global manufacturing, financial, HR, order management, purchasing, customer service, and other processes
• Individual financial advisers own their customer relationships	• Business units all support global chemical research, development, and sales
• Financial advisers customize their interactions with customers	• Centralized management with matrixed business unit/process/geographical management
• Financial advisers in 630 offices exercise local autonomy within bounds of their responsibilities	• Centralized process design implemented through ERP and corporate process owners
• Total Merrill platform provides shared access to technology and data	• Centrally mandated, single instance of key databases
• IT organization provides centralized technology standards	• IT decisions made through central shared IT services organization
Diversification	**Replication**
JM Family Enterprises	**TD Banknorth**
• Few shared customers or suppliers	• Few, if any, shared customers
• Mostly independent transactions with intercompany transactions at arm's length	• Banks record independent customer transactions aggregated centrally
• Unique operations across business units	• Banks decide locally how to serve their customers while implementing company practices
• Autonomous business unit heads reporting directly to CEO; arm's-length transactions between business units	• Growing companywide standard processes to increase efficiencies and limit risk
• Business unit control over business process design except for shared procurement, HR, financial, dealer, and corporate services	• New business processes designed centrally
• Few data standards across units	• Data locally owned; standard data definitions accompanying process standard implementations
• Shared IT services to realize economies of scale	• Assimilating existing IT systems of individual banks into central systems

Business process integration — High (top), Low (bottom)

Business process standardization — Low (left), High (right)

saturated, the company is preparing to grow through acquisitions—a common characteristic of Diversification companies. Because JMFE's business units are run autonomously, each of them has an operating model capturing its individual integration and standardization requirements. By building a foundation for execution to support their individual operating models, these business units contribute profitable growth to JMFE.

The organizing logic for Diversification companies is based on synergies from related, but not integrated, business units. Business units might create demand for one another or increase the company's brand recognition, which generates enterprisewide value despite autonomous management. Companies with a Diversification model may pursue economies of scale through shared services, but they typically grow through the success of the individual business units and acquisitions of other related businesses.

Coordination: Seamless Access to Shared Data

Coordination calls for high levels of integration but little standardization of processes. Business units in a Coordination company share one or more of the following: customers, products, suppliers, and partners. The benefits of integration can include integrated customer service, cross-selling, and transparency across supply chain processes. While key business processes are integrated, however, business units have unique operations, often demanding unique capabilities.

For companies with a Coordination model, low cost is usually not the primary driver in companywide decisions. Autonomous business heads execute their processes in the most efficient manner possible, but corporate directives and negotiations focus on providing the best service to the customer. Strong central management defines the need for cooperation. Successful companies rely on incentive systems and management training to encourage companywide thinking at the business unit level. (See the Coordination quadrant of figure 2-1.)

Merrill Lynch, one of the world's largest financial services companies, is composed of three major business units: the Global Markets & Investment Banking Group, Merrill Lynch Investment Managers, and Global Private Client. Its Global Private Client (GPC) business provides an example of a Coordination operating model (figure 2-2). GPC delivers wealth management products and services to individuals and small businesses through more than 14,000 financial advisers in approximately 630 offices around the world. While financial advisers each serve their individual customers, their services are integrated through what's called the Total Merrill platform, which gives all advisers access to the full range of Merrill products: commission- and fee-based investment accounts, credit products, banking services, cash management and credit cards, trust and generational planning, consumer and small-business lending, retirement services, and insurance products.[5]

GPC focuses on delivering comprehensive, innovative solutions to meet the financial needs of its target customers. These customers want to do business with Merrill Lynch through a variety of channels, such as the telephone call center, the Internet, and advice-based interactions with financial advisers. In addition, customers want access to non-Merrill products. GPC's operating model, therefore, coordinates services to its customers by providing integrated access to products across customers and integrated access to customer data across products and channels. Such service requires highly standardized product and customer data, but it allows financial advisers to customize their individual interactions to the needs of their customers. Merrill Lynch calls its model providing "all things to some people," and customized service is important to retaining high-value customers.[6]

Merrill Lynch's GPC grows by increasing the number of financial advisers who, with their access to product data, can identify and then serve more customers. GPC also regularly innovates to expand its product line, recently adding products such as new credit cards and loan management services. These new services help GPC provide a strong portfolio of products as it seeks to retain its ability to provide a full range of services to clients.

GPC's standard technology platform and access to shared business data enable the company to productively employ the largest number of financial advisers in the industry. These financial advisers have the industry's best revenue per adviser, earnings per adviser, and assets per adviser.[7]

Like GPC, most companies in the Coordination quadrant can grow by extending their reach to defined customer segments in new markets. They can also increase services to meet new, but related, customer demands. By integrating, but not standardizing, product lines or functions, the Coordination model fosters process expertise while enhancing customer service. This expertise attracts new customers and sells more products to existing customers, thus enabling profitable growth.

Replication: Standardized Independence

Replication models grant autonomy to business units but run operations in a highly standardized fashion. In a Replication model the company's success is dependent on efficient, repeatable business processes rather than on shared customer relationships. The business units are not dependent on one another's transactions or data; the success of the company as a whole is dependent on global innovation and the efficiency of all business units implementing a set of standardized business processes. Accordingly, business unit managers have limited discretion over business process design, even though they operate independently of other business units. McDonald's, like other franchise operations, provides a clear reference point for a Replication model. (See the Replication quadrant of figure 2-1.)

TD Banknorth, one of the thirty-five largest commercial banking companies in the United States, also provides an example of a Replication model (figure 2-2). Over the past decade, the company has grown by a factor of ten from a small community bank to the largest bank headquartered in New England. TD Banknorth's core strategy is to grow through acquisitions of community banks with customer-focused corporate cultures. The company adds value by introducing economies of scale and providing its banks' customers with new and improved products.[8]

Founded in Vermont in 1824, TD Banknorth grew with the objective of understanding its customers better than anyone else. As a result, each local bank developed its own processes and infrastructures to meet the perceived needs of its specific customers. But when John Petrey became the company's CIO in September 2001, he set out to integrate and standardize its information technology. Petrey created standardized processes for bringing new banks onto TD Banknorth's foundation.

These new standardized processes are converting TD Banknorth from a Diversification model, with independent operations in each of the company's banks, to a Replication model, in which banks are run independently but with the same IT infrastructure and a set of standardized core processes. To facilitate this transition, a new Enterprise Projects Committee, headed by COO Peter Verrill, reviews projects for their strategic impact in light of the company's focus on developing synergies across its banks. While Banknorth looks for the efficiencies and predictability of standardized processes, however, it also aims to preserve the image of a community bank by retaining local decision making wherever feasible.

Many Replication companies grow through acquisition like TD Banknorth, but most Replication companies can also build new businesses from scratch. Whether companies are growing organically or through acquisition, the Replication model helps them increase profits when management quickly installs its standardized practices and technology foundation into a new unit and then allows a local manager to build the business.

Unification: Standardized, Integrated Processes

When organizational units are tightly integrated around a standardized set of processes, companies benefit from a Unification model. Companies applying this model find little benefit in business unit autonomy. They maximize efficiencies and customer services by presenting integrated data and driving variability out of business processes.

Unification companies typically have integrated supply chains, creating interdependence between distributed business units. These business units share transaction data, often including global customer and supplier data. Standardized processes support global integration and increase efficiency. The Unification operating model often benefits from implementation of large packaged systems to support company standardization and integration requirements. (See the Unification quadrant in figure 2-1.)

The Dow Chemical Company has adopted a Unification model for its core chemicals-manufacturing business.[9] Founded in 1897, Dow Chemical develops and sells innovative chemical, plastic, and agricultural products and services to customers in more than 175 countries around the world. From 1994 to 2004, despite a downturn in the market, Dow nearly doubled its revenues while growing its employee base less than 10 percent—a productivity improvement of 8 percent per year. Management attributes much of the company's success to its well-tuned globally integrated processes (figure 2-2).

Managers at Dow estimate that approximately 60 percent of the company's work processes are standardized. For example, financial work processes are common around the globe. Manufacturing has common processes for building plants, driven in part by the need for those facilities to be highly cost effective and environmentally secure. Standardized human resource processes allow Dow to do performance management and to plan salaries and incentives around the globe in three weeks, equitably and transparently, even taking into account multiple currencies and differing rates of inflation. Finally, some supply chain work processes (e.g., order to cash) are globally standardized; others (e.g., planning and scheduling) are specific to particular products or regions.

Dow constantly reengineers processes to introduce greater standardization and automation, as appropriate. These efforts are intended, first and foremost, to cut costs, but they also increase quality, safety, and security—other important organizational objectives. Dow invests substantial resources in understanding the costs of its processes and the impacts of its improvement efforts.

Dow sustains its integration and standardization through global systems, such as SAP's enterprise resource planning system, and through a management structure that assigns owners to the various global processes. Five of Dow's eight global processes are housed in a shared services organization that includes IT, purchasing, supply chain services, and customer service (including e-business), along with expertise on six-sigma and work processes. Dow's matrixed management structure, in which managers often report to product and process heads or to product and geographic heads, further encourages global integration.

Unification companies invariably have highly centralized management environments. Management drives out inefficiencies and then grows the company by leveraging economies of scale. Since minimizing variation is key to driving efficiencies, Unification is best suited to companies whose products and services are largely commodities. Companies more focused on innovation may find that the costs of standardization outweigh its benefits.

Applying the Operating Model

An operating model represents a general vision of how a company will enable and execute strategies. Each operating model presents different opportunities and challenges for growth. For example, the need to integrate business processes, as in Coordination and Unification operating models, makes acquisition more challenging because the new company must reconcile disparate data definitions. On the other hand, the process integration of the Coordination and Unification models facilitates organic growth through expansion into new markets or extensions of current product lines.

Process standardization, as in Unification and Replication models, enables growth through a rip-and-replace approach to acquisitions. When the acquisition is intended to create a mirror image, a company can replace the systems and processes of the acquired

FIGURE 2-3

Different operating models position companies for different types of growth

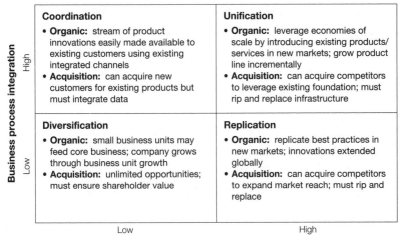

Business process integration

High

Coordination
- **Organic:** stream of product innovations easily made available to existing customers using existing integrated channels
- **Acquisition:** can acquire new customers for existing products but must integrate data

Unification
- **Organic:** leverage economies of scale by introducing existing products/ services in new markets; grow product line incrementally
- **Acquisition:** can acquire competitors to leverage existing foundation; must rip and replace infrastructure

Low

Diversification
- **Organic:** small business units may feed core business; company grows through business unit growth
- **Acquisition:** unlimited opportunities; must ensure shareholder value

Replication
- **Organic:** replicate best practices in new markets; innovations extended globally
- **Acquisition:** can acquire competitors to expand market reach; must rip and replace

Low   High

Business process standardization

© 2005 MIT Sloan Center for Information Systems Research. Used with permission.

business with its own. But both the Unification and Replication models depend on leveraging processes already in place. Neither model offers much leverage when a company chooses to expand into synergistic, but operationally distinct, lines of business.

The Diversification model imposes fewer constraints on the organic growth of individual business units and fewer challenges in an acquisition. But it also leverages fewer capabilities than the other models, thus offering fewer opportunities to create shareholder value. Figure 2-3 summarizes the growth opportunities presented by each of the operating models.

Deploying Operating Models at Different Organizational Levels

Although most companies can identify processes fitting every operating model, they need to select a single operating model to guide management thinking and system implementations. Management can then organize responsibilities for business units and IT based on principles about how the company will operate most of the time. One way companies respond to conflicting demands is to adopt different operating models at different organizational levels. For example, a company with a Diversification model, like JM Family Enterprises, often adopts different models in its business units.

Johnson & Johnson (J&J) has long operated in the Diversification quadrant. General managers in the company's more than 200 operating companies have always had significant autonomy, and for most of J&J's 100-plus years of existence, analysts believed that this decentralized management style was key to the company's success. But as major global customers increasingly demand integration across multiple business units, J&J responds by introducing new organizational levels that can provide shared customer data across subsets of related business units.[10]

J&J's U.S. pharmaceutical group applies a Coordination model, presenting a single face to health-care professionals. In Europe, its Janssen Pharmaceutical Products applies a Replication model, providing low-cost, standardized processes for drug marketing, delivery, and monitoring. Having different operating models at different organizational levels allows J&J to meet the multiple objectives of large, complex companies while keeping organizational design reasonably simple at the individual operating company level.

Many companies in the Diversification quadrant, including DuPont, Citicorp, and General Electric, have multiple organizational levels, each adopting a different operating model so that it can simultaneously meet the company's and its own business objectives.

Transforming to a New Operating Model

An operating model helps define the range of strategic initiatives a company can readily pursue. As long as the operating model presents attractive options, it provides a stable approach for delivering goods and services. If a company determines that its existing operating model is not well suited to its market realities, the company must shift to a new operating model. Shifting from one operating model to another is transformational. A transformation disrupts a company, imposing new ways of thinking and behaving.[11] But while companies would not want to regularly introduce new operating models, such changes are sometimes necessary.

From Diversification to Unification: a European packaging company

A European packaging company recognized a need to change operating models in the late 1990s.[12] At the time, the company was organized into separate country-based business units, each of which was responsible for its own operations. Different countries had different enterprise resource planning (ERP) systems, order management processes, invoice formats, and even pricing. Each country made its own decisions about IT systems and data standards, which was a slow, inefficient, and expensive way to do business. Alarmingly, management discovered some corporate customers were taking the same order to multiple organizations to drive down the price by bidding one country-based unit against others!

The management team decided its key operations were sales, order processing, new product introductions, and after-sales service. Management decided it could accomplish those operations better with a Unification model than with a Diversification model. The company didn't need to adopt a new strategy—it was still delivering the same products to the same customers. The change in operating model was designed to help it deliver products and services faster, better, and more efficiently.

To transform its operating model, management replaced the different order management systems in each country with a central ERP system and process. The countries now enter orders through a browser interface with one product list, price list, and order management system for the entire business.

The company's new operating model dramatically reduced order management cycle time, lowered operational costs, and increased business flexibility and agility. In the old operating model, adding a product with a new pricing structure required updating 15 different systems, which could take weeks. In the new system, one central change is made, usually in a matter of hours. But the new operating model had dramatic effects on the power structure of the company, making the transition difficult. In the old model, a country manager could, within limits, make independent decisions about products, pricing, and promotions. That authority was greatly reduced, and local managers naturally resisted the change.

Shifting from Diversification to Unification introduces traumatic organizational change. As companies attempt to increase standardization and integration, they obsolete existing systems, processes, and organizational structures and roles. Successful transformations of this kind are costly, time consuming, risky—and sometimes necessary. As we saw with the packaging company, the rewards of the change can be substantial.

From Unification to Diversification: Schneider National

Schneider National, a large, privately held trucking company, built a strong Unification model in the early 1990s.[13] Schneider had highly standardized and integrated operations processes and systems built around a centralized management model in which most employees were based in Green Bay, Wisconsin. The company had long been recognized as an industry leader in the effective use of IT. Schneider was the first trucking company to implement satellite tracking systems and then the first to integrate its tracking systems with both operations and customer service applications. But management decided in the early nineties that many of the United States' 50,000 trucking companies were dropping prices and pushing down margins throughout the industry. Any person with a truck could go into the trucking business, making it increasingly difficult for Schneider to grow profitably.

Responding to the requests of some of the company's key customers, Schneider decided to offer logistics services. Management recognized that a new logistics business could not leverage the company's existing foundation for execution. Trucking demands centralization, standardization, and integration to serve customers who need reliable service delivery and accompanying information. Schneider intended to provide localized, customized logistics services, managed by logistics representatives who would sit at customer sites and access local databases. Thus, the operating platform that had regularly enabled innovation in the trucking business was not a good fit for logistics. So when Schneider launched the logistics business, it did so with a new and separate management structure and segregated IT processes and operations.

Over time, Schneider has found synergies between its two businesses. In particular, the trucking business has benefited from some of the newer technologies introduced to support logistics. But Schneider has two foundations for execution: one for the Unification operating model of the trucking business and one for the Replication operating model of the logistics business. As a whole, Schneider has a Diversification model with some shared infrastructure and services to benefit both businesses. Companies with a core business adopting a Unification model, like Schneider, may run out of opportunities to leverage that core. A Diversification model provides opportunities to feed the core business.

The Operating Model as Company Vision

Focusing on the operating model rather than on individual business strategies gives a company better guidance for developing IT and business process capabilities. This stable foundation enables IT to become a proactive—rather than reactive—force in identifying future strategic initiatives. In selecting an operating model, management defines the role of business process standardization and integration in the company's daily decisions and tasks.

The operating model concept requires that management put a stake in the ground and declare which business processes will distinguish a company from its competitors. A poor choice of operating model—one that is not viable in a given market—will have dire consequences. But not choosing an operating model is just as risky. Without a clear operating model, management careens from one market opportunity to the next, unable to leverage reusable capabilities. With a declared operating model, management builds capabilities that can drive profitable growth.

Because the choice of an operating model guides development of business and IT capabilities, it determines which strategic opportunities the company should—and should not—seize. In other words, the operating model, once in place, becomes a driver of business strategy. In addition, the required architecture—as well as the management thinking, practices, policies, and processes characteristic of each operating model—is different from one operating model to another. As a result, the operating model could be a key driver of the design of separate organizational units.

We encourage senior managers to debate their company's operating model. This debate can force managers to articulate a vision for how the company will operate and how those operations will distinguish the company in the marketplace. In clarifying this vision, management provides critical direction for building a foundation for execution.

3

Implement the
Operating Model via
Enterprise Architecture

IN 1884 Sarah Winchester, heiress to the Winchester Repeating Arms Co. fortune, bought a six-room house in Santa Clara while it was still under construction. She quickly discarded the building plans and instead met with her foreman every morning to describe the work she wanted done that day. With no master plan, she kept twenty-two carpenters at work, year round—for thirty-six years! The house had three elevators, forty-seven fireplaces, rooms built around rooms, staircases leading to nowhere, doors opening to blank walls, doors opening to steep drops to the lawn below, and a variety of other curiosities. The house had every type of heating technology available. The design is so complex that no one knows for sure the number of rooms in the house—though most counters agree it's around 160.[1]

Crazy as it seems, the architecture of the Winchester House is perfectly designed to meet the needs of its owner. Sarah Winchester wanted to confound the spirits of the men who had been killed by the Winchester rifle and might want to harm her. As companies cobble together their systems and processes—year after year, often for more than thirty-six years—they run the risk of having an architecture much like Winchester House. But since few companies are battling evil spirits, a confounding architecture may just be the result of poor management, rather than the intended chaos of Sarah Winchester.

Responding to market opportunities is critical to any business—particularly in new areas where the company must establish a presence and a value proposition quickly. For example, many companies sprang into action in response to the Internet boom in early 2000. One such company was Manheim Auctions, a division of Cox Communications and the largest automobile auction company in the world. In February 2000 Manheim Auctions launched Manheim Interactive, a business-to-business Internet company. By the end of its first year, Manheim Interactive had 275 employees dedicated to rapidly building new, innovative technology-based tools to help dealers, manufacturers, and other automobile marketers manage the used-car remarketing process. The focus on rapid introduction of a stream of new products and services superseded architectural concerns. Short-term, Manheim Interactive generated the desired results from its efforts, but eventually, management had to examine the underlying architecture of its IT and business process capabilities. As Steve Crawford, director of software development at Manheim Interactive, explains, "The ability to always quickly respond eventually became a problem. We became very good at scrambling to meet demands very quickly. But that has a cost and eventually we just said, 'Okay, we're out of magic dust now. We need to rethink.'"[2]

Companies looking to build a strong foundation for execution need more detail than the operating model provides—they need an enterprise architecture to guide their efforts. The operating model outlines, in general terms, the expectations for integration and standardization across business units; the enterprise architecture delineates the key processes, systems, and data composing the core of a company's operations. Enterprise architecture directs the digitization of the foundation for execution.

Unfortunately the term *architecture* has acquired a negative connotation in some companies. Many companies have questioned the value of their architecture initiatives. Some of those initiatives are viewed as IT ivory towers that are isolated from business reality. The chief architect of a large telecommunications company confirmed this idea, saying, "Architectures, like fondue sets and sandwich makers, are rarely used. We occasionally dig them out and wonder why we ever spent the money on them."[3]

In this chapter we discuss how to make enterprise architecture a powerful management tool for aligning business and technology initiatives throughout a company. We define what we mean by the term *enterprise architecture*. We then show how four different organizations draw and describe their architecture. In doing so, we explain how companies convert the fairly general vision of the operating model into a guide for their business processes and IT capabilities.

The Enterprise Architecture

Enterprise architecture is the organizing logic for business processes and IT infrastructure reflecting the integration and standardization requirements of the company's operating model.

Many companies attack the enterprise architecture exercise with lots of drawings and analysis of both existing and hoped-for systems capabilities. But massive analytical efforts do not focus resources on what matters. The key to effective enterprise architecture is to identify the processes, data, technologies, and customer interfaces that take the operating model from vision to reality.

The key elements of enterprise architecture are different for each of the four operating models. For JM Family Enterprises, which runs its business units autonomously, the key element of enterprise architecture is its shared technology environment. For

Distinguishing Between Enterprise Architecture and IT Architecture

The enterprise architecture core diagrams we describe in this chapter are focused on communicating the high-level business process and IT requirements of a company's operating model. They do not provide the necessary detail to map out technical or process design requirements. The IT unit typically addresses four levels of architecture below the enterprise architecture: business process architecture (the activities or tasks composing major business processes identified by the business process owners); data or information architecture (shared data definitions); applications architecture (individual applications and their interfaces); and technology architecture (infrastructure services and the technology standards they are built on).

The term *enterprise architecture* can be confusing because the IT unit in some companies refers to one of these architectures—or the set of all four architectures—as the enterprise architecture. Our use of the term refers to the high-level logic for business processes and IT capabilities.

For the most part, non-IT people need not be involved in the development of the detailed technical and applications architectures

Merrill Lynch's Global Private Client, which works to meet the total financial needs of each individual customer, the key element of enterprise architecture is the customer's data and the interface that captures and accesses that data. For Dow Chemical, which prides itself in the cost-effectiveness and safety of its manufacturing and distribution processes, the key element of enterprise guiding development of technical capabilities. However, they need to provide enough detail on how they will execute processes, and what data those processes depend on, for the IT unit to develop current solutions meeting long-term needs. A high-level enterprise architecture creates shared understanding of how a company will operate, but the convergence of people, process, and technology necessary to implement that architecture demands shared understanding of processes and data at a more detailed level.

The IT unit will develop far more detailed architectures of applications, data and information, and technology.[a] When these drawings elaborate on enterprise architecture, they have considerable long-term value because they provide the long-term context for immediate solutions. When IT units attempt to develop detailed architectures without a clear understanding of the company's enterprise architecture, they may have developed the equivalent of a fondue pot—an ornament rather than a tool.

a. Detailed architecture development conducted within the IT unit is an important element of building a foundation for execution. However, it is outside the scope of this book. A variety of resources describe the IT unit's role in enterprise architecture. Some highlight one specific type of architecture (e.g., information or application architecture). For an overview of the IT unit's role, see Steven H. Spewak, *Enterprise Architecture Planning: Developing a Blueprint for Data, Applications, and Technology* (New York: Wiley, 1993) or John A. Zachman, "A Framework for Information Systems Architecture," *IBM Systems Journal* 26, no. 3 (1987): 276–292.

architecture is the set of standardized processes and shared data built on its single instance of an ERP system. TD Banknorth's success depends on implementation of a shared technology and business process environment.

All four of these companies have legacy systems and processes that aren't a perfect fit with current technologies and business goals. But these companies understand their operating models, and they capture the critical components of their operating model in their enterprise architecture. They use their architecture to continually improve their foundation for execution.

Encapsulating Enterprise Architecture in a Core Diagram

While the architecture for a new building is captured in blueprints, enterprise architecture is often represented in principles, policies, and technology choices. Thus, the concept can be difficult for managers to get their arms around. We have found that a simple picture, which we refer to as the "core diagram," helps managers debate and eventually come to understand their company's enterprise architecture. This simple one-page picture is a high-level view of the processes, data, and technologies constituting the desired foundation for execution. The core diagram provides a rallying point for managers responsible for building out and exploiting the enterprise architecture. It also has implications for the design of organizational roles and structures. Although these structural requirements are not usually captured in the core diagram, roles and reporting relationships also need to be aligned with the enterprise architecture.

All companies have entrenched legacy systems that are the accumulation of years of IT-enabled business projects. Intentionally or not, the resulting capability locks in assumptions about internal and external relationships and business process definitions. The role of the one-page core diagram is to help facilitate discussions between business and IT managers to clarify requirements for the company's foundation for execution and then communicate the vision.

Although different companies take different approaches to developing their core diagram, all highlight key components of their foundation for execution. We have observed four common elements in enterprise architecture core diagrams:

1. *Core business processes.* This small set of enterprise processes defines the stable set of company-wide capabilities the company needs to execute its operating model and respond to market opportunities.

2. *Shared data driving core processes.* This data may be the customer files shared across the product lines of a full-service financial services institution or the master supplier and item data shared across the business units of a company instituting a global supply chain.

3. *Key linking and automation technologies.* These technologies include software known as "middleware" (i.e., a linking technology), which enables integration of applications and access to shared data, and major software packages, such as ERP systems (i.e., an automation technology). Key technologies also include portals providing standardized access to systems and data or a customer interface distinguishing a company from its competitors. Electronic interfaces to key stakeholder groups (employees, customers, partners, suppliers) also might appear on an enterprise architecture core diagram.

4. *Key customers.* These show the major customer groups (e.g., channels or segments) served by the foundation for execution.

The key elements highlighted in a core diagram are specific to that company's operating model. Thus, we tend to see similarities between the core diagrams of companies adopting the same operating model. We will now describe characteristics of the enterprise architecture for the four operating models. To illustrate an architecture for each, we will start with a company example and then provide a general template and steps for designing the core diagram. We will look at Delta Air Lines, Carlson Companies, MetLife, and ING DIRECT.

Enterprise Architecture for a Unification Model

In a Unification operating model, both integration and standardization of business processes are required to serve different key customer types. Technology is used to link as well as to automate processes. Delta Air Lines has arguably the best foundation for execution of any of the full-service airlines.

In 1997 Leo Mullin became CEO of Delta Air Lines, the United States' third-largest airline in terms of revenues and passenger miles flown.[4] Mullin quickly learned that Delta's IT capability had been constructed in response to a failed outsourcing effort. Unhappy with the outsourcer's services, each of Delta's seventeen functional units had effectively built its own IT capability. The firm had as many IT platforms as it had functions, and those platforms were not capable of communicating with one another. The predictable outcome was that Delta's ticket agents, reservation agents, gate agents, baggage handlers, and others often lacked the information they needed to do their jobs—frustrating both customers and employees. Negotiating the core diagram helped Delta's management and IT staff reach a common understanding of the capabilities the company would develop to support future strategies.

As a first step in clarifying the vision, the management team defined four core processes: customer experience, operational pipeline, business reflexes, and employee relationship management (figure 3-1). The customer experience identified all the ways Delta touched its customers. The operational pipeline was concerned with loading, moving, unloading, and maintaining planes. Business reflexes focused on how the company made money: scheduling, pricing, and financial processes. Employee relationship management encompassed processes involved in the scheduling, compensation, and development of Delta's highly mobile workforce.

Once the management team agreed on the core processes, they identified nine types of data critical to process execution. These nine databases are shown in the center of the core diagram. Surrounding the shared data in this diagram is the Delta nervous

FIGURE 3-1

Delta Air Lines core diagram

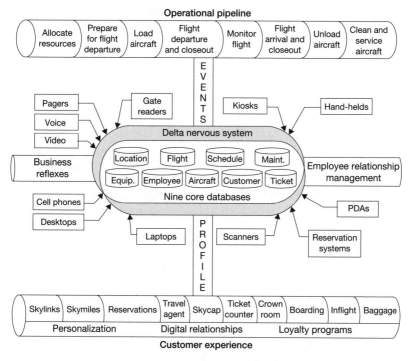

Source: Adapted from Delta Air Lines documents. Used with permission.

system—software that accesses the company's shared data for real-time updates. The Delta nervous system is designed to make data available to customers, employees, and the company's core processes on a need-to-know basis. This linking technology is a key element to enabling Delta's highly standardized and integrated operating model.

In early 2001, Mullin noted that technology and process improvements resulting from enterprise architecture efforts had shifted Delta from regularly appearing in last place on key performance indicators (in 1997) to being the only airline that was consistently in the top three on the most important metrics: on-time performance,

lost baggage, and customer complaints. Delta's enterprise architecture, however, was not sufficient to save the company from
bankruptcy after difficult times hit the major airlines in late 2001.
Delta's current financial woes are a sobering reminder that a foundation for execution cannot sustain a company if its market strategy is not viable.

The top half of figure 3-2 identifies the process for designing
the enterprise architecture core diagram of a Unification company. For the core diagram of a Unification company, three elements are required. Start by identifying the key customers (i.e.,
segments and/or channels) the company serves. Next, list the key
processes to be standardized and integrated. Then identify the
shared data needed to better integrate processes and serve customers. Finally, if there are key technologies that either automate

FIGURE 3-2

Unification core diagram

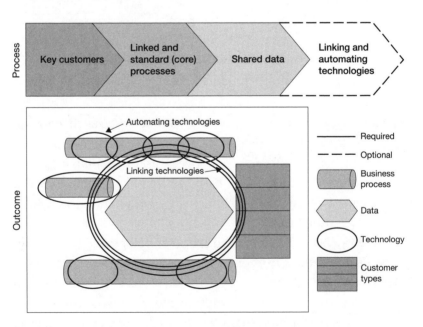

© 2005 MIT Sloan Center for Information Systems Research and IMD. Used with permission.

or link processes, these can be shown as well (optional elements are identified with a dashed outline in the figure).

The bottom half of figure 3-2 presents the enterprise architecture core diagram of a company with a Unification operating model. The diagram reflects a highly standardized and integrated environment with standard processes accessing shared data to make products and services available to customers. The core diagram may or may not show key technologies, depending on the significance of any particular technology to the management vision.

Enterprise Architecture for a Diversification Model

The Diversification operating model is the opposite of the Unification model and entails both low integration and low standardization. Each business is run more or less independently, although there can be opportunities for shared services across the company.

Carlson Companies, a $20 billion company in the marketing, hospitality, and travel business, has a Diversification model.[5] Carlson's portfolio includes Radisson Hotels, T.G.I. Friday's restaurants, Carlson Marketing Group, Carlson Wagonlit Travel, Radisson Seven Seas Cruises, and the Gold Points Reward Network.

Even though these companies are run autonomously, Carlson has captured cost savings and synergies with a world-class shared services capability, which was awarded the 2004 International Productivity and Quality Council's award for the "best mature shared services organization." Carlson's Shared Services organization is set up to operate as a business, offering IT and financial services with plans to offer more.

Carlson's enterprise architecture core diagram emphasizes technologies, reflecting management's belief that technical infrastructure services should be shared while business units retain control over local business processes and IT applications. Carlson's Diversification model calls for a lean core diagram at the overall company level. Thus, the core diagram capturing Carlson's enterprise architecture shows only shared services and the technical infrastructure needed to provide them (figure 3-3).[6]

FIGURE 3-3

Carlson's core diagram

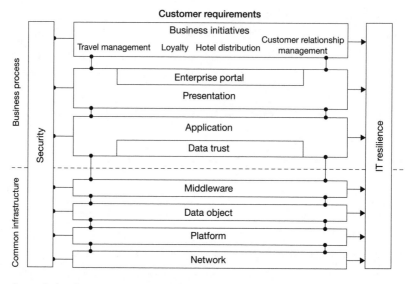

Source: Carlson Companies. Used with permission.

An extreme example of Diversification would be a total lack of an enterprise architecture—a company intending to have no synergies across its businesses. More often, companies adopting the Diversification operating model establish economies of scale through a shared technology platform. These shared technologies are the key element of the enterprise architecture core diagram. Shared technologies and services often include data centers, the telecommunications network, offshore systems development and maintenance capability, centralized vendor negotiations, and help desks. Diversification companies that value other shared services might also represent some standard processes or even shared data in their core diagram, particularly if a subset of business units is sharing data but hasn't created a formal structure to manage it (figure 3-4).

When designing a Diversification model core diagram, start with the technologies that can be shared to provide economies of

FIGURE 3-4

Diversification core diagram

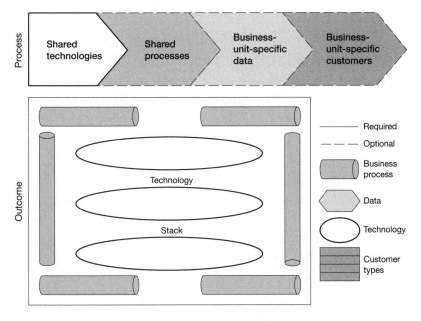

© 2005 MIT Sloan Center for Information Systems Research and IMD. Used with permission.

scale, standardization, or other benefits. Incorporate the remaining elements—key customer types, business processes, and data—only when needed for the operating model. For example, some Diversification companies require a standardized process and data for financial reporting, risk management, and compliance across their business units. Providing a single interface to common customers in a Diversification company, however, is rare.

Enterprise Architecture for a Coordination Model

The Coordination model provides integrated service to each key customer group. The integration results from sharing key data across the business units to present a common face to the customer. Because of their wide range of distinctive products, many large financial services institutions, such as MetLife, have adopted a Coordination model. Coordination allows companies to integrate untold numbers of products or processes without forcing standardization.

MetLife is a leading provider of insurance and other financial services to millions of individual and institutional customers throughout the United States.[7] Through its subsidiaries and affiliates, MetLife offers life insurance, annuities, automobile and homeowner's insurance, and retail banking services to individuals, as well as group insurance, reinsurance, and retirement and savings products and services to corporations and other institutions. Outside the United States, the MetLife companies have direct insurance operations in Asia Pacific, Latin America, and Europe.

Following a series of mergers in the 1990s, MetLife's management worked to reduce costs through increased standardization of business functions and common processes, such as finance, human resources, and regulatory compliance. But like most insurance companies, MetLife had built systems supporting key operations, such as underwriting, payments, workflow, and account origination, into individual insurance products. Extracting processes from individual products was a slow, costly proposition. More important, individual products and product lines required specialized knowledge, thereby limiting opportunities for standardization across products and business units.

Accordingly, MetLife focused on developing a strategy and operating model to provide integrated customer service across products—a Coordination model. This integrated view of the customer required extracting customer information from individual products and making it centrally available. MetLife's enterprise architecture core diagram reflects the importance of integrated data by locating at the center of its diagram an integration hub—software developed in-house using commercial packages to access customer data from existing systems (figure 3-5).

MetLife is now building a centralized data store to hold customer data and other information separate from individual insurance

FIGURE 3-5

MetLife's core diagram

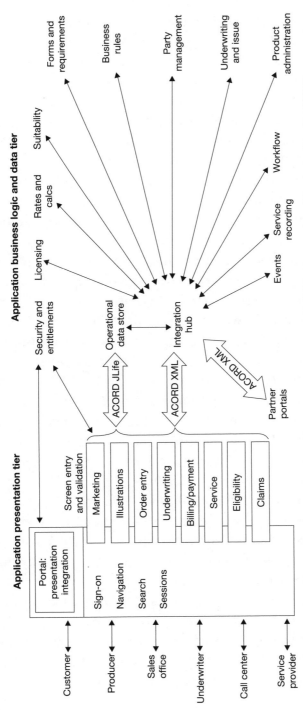

Note: ACORD JLife and ACORD XML are insurance industry technical standards. JLife is a data model; XML is a language for real-time transactions. See ACORD, "Global Insurance Standards," http://www.acord.org/standards/LifeMain.aspx.

Source: Adapted from MetLife documents. Used with permission.

products. This data store is a long-term project, so, as it is being developed, the integration hub accesses data embedded in legacy applications and provides exclusive access to the customer information file. Subject to MetLife's privacy and other compliance requirements, most stakeholders gain access to the data using a standardized portal, shown on the left-hand side of the diagram. A separate electronic link to the integration hub provides MetLife's partners (labs, brokerages, regulatory agencies, etc.) with access to certain company systems and data. The processes listed on the right-hand side of the core diagram are examples of the systems and processes the integration hub accesses. Unlike the processes in the Delta core diagram (and any Unification model), most insurance processes will not be standardized across all business units or products. However, *within* individual business units and product lines, MetLife is moving toward a Unification model to capture potential efficiencies and enable predictability.

The enterprise architecture core diagram for the Coordination operating model encapsulates a company's integration emphasis and thus focuses on shared data (figure 3-6). Often, the core diagram will also highlight important technology that depicts how stakeholders can access that data. Because most processes in a Coordination model are unique, it is less important to show them on the core diagram. However, it can be useful to show at least some of the processes to be coordinated.

When designing a Coordination model core diagram, start with the key customers (e.g., segments and channels) to be shared across business units. For MetLife this was a combination of internal and external groups that tie into the portal. Next, identify the subset of the company data that must be shared across the business units to serve key customers. Then, identify any technology that is key to the data integration. It is not essential to reflect the technology, but it is usually helpful for business and IT managers to understand, at a high level, the key to data integration. Finally, consider whether to include business process elements.

FIGURE 3-6

Coordination core diagram

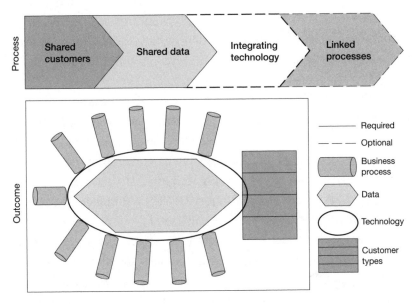

© 2005 MIT Sloan Center for Information Systems Research and IMD. Used with permission.

Enterprise Architecture for a Replication Model

Replication operating models are successful when key processes are standardized across the company and supported by automating technology. This Replication allows rapid expansion and scalability of the business, as demonstrated by ING DIRECT.

ING DIRECT, a subsidiary of the Dutch financial services giant ING Groep, was founded in 1997 as a telephone bank in Canada.[8] One of the fastest-growing companies in history, ING DIRECT is a direct-to-customer operation, offering simple banking products to 13 million customers of nine country-based bank organizations in Europe, North America, and Australia. Customers access ING DIRECT via the Internet, mail, or phone. There are no branches and few ATMs. Products are transparent and easy to understand with no fees or minimum deposits and simple features with no confusing fine print or complex rules. ING DIRECT has only a limited number of product offerings, including savings accounts, simple mortgages, certificates of deposit, and a handful of mutual funds. The company's low fees, high returns, and multiple channels appeal to a broad range of customers.

ING DIRECT's country-based businesses operate autonomously, but they share a common set of standardized business solutions as well as standardized technical infrastructure components. ING DIRECT selects business solutions on behalf of all business units with a joint request-for-proposal process reflecting shared requirements. Architectural fit and global support are key requirements. Country managers can decide which modules they would like to adopt, but they cannot introduce customized local solutions for key components (although some customized solutions are allowed when it's unavoidable). Module reuse keeps operational costs low (0.43% of assets, as compared to 2.5% for a typical full-service bank) and allows the company to offer higher savings rates and lower-cost loans.[9]

ING DIRECT's enterprise architecture core diagram reflects its Replication operating model (figure 3-7). The modularity of ING DIRECT's systems is highlighted by seven service groupings. Even external services, such as prospecting and publishing agency reports, are designed as modules interfacing with the ING DIRECT infrastructure. Customer relationship services allow each country-based bank to manage its customer data and interactions. These modules are distinct from common business service modules, which manage interactions between systems as transactions are processed. For example, when a new customer signs up for an ING DIRECT product, common business service modules update the customer information file, contact history file, and customer relationship management system. These common business services also record a customer's deposit and process the transaction. A different set of services—the channel services—connect back-end systems to systems that communicate with customers.

FIGURE 3-7

ING DIRECT's core diagram

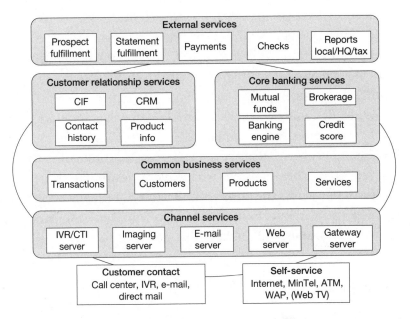

Note: CIF (customer information file), CRM (customer relationship management), IVR (interactive voice response), CTI (computer-telephony integration), WAP (wireless access point).

Source: Adapted from ING Direct documents. Used with permission.

ING DIRECT's service modules digitize standardized processes across its businesses, thereby enabling ING DIRECT's Replication operating model. By identifying major service categories, the enterprise architecture core diagram helps management understand existing capabilities and target new opportunities. The core diagram shows no data because the nine country-based banks do not share data (each bank serves its own customers—regardless of where they are at the time they seek service). Instead, the core diagram highlights the key process components, which management refers to as "services."

Replication operating models revolve around standardized processes. Thus an enterprise architecture core diagram will show key standard processes and, in most cases, the key technologies enabling those processes (figure 3-8). Data rarely appears in the core diagram because Replication companies don't typically share data across business units. To improve the economics of Replication these companies automate key processes, often creating reusable business modules (shown as business processes surrounded by technology in figure 3-8). The enterprise architecture core diagram also typically shows shared technologies linking the standardized processes.

When designing a Replication model core diagram, start with the key processes to be standardized and replicated across the business units. Next, identify the technologies automating those key processes. Then consider what linking technologies, if any, can be shared across the business units. It is not usually necessary in a Replication model to share data or identify key customers. Instead, each business unit makes those decisions locally.

FIGURE 3-8

Replication core diagram

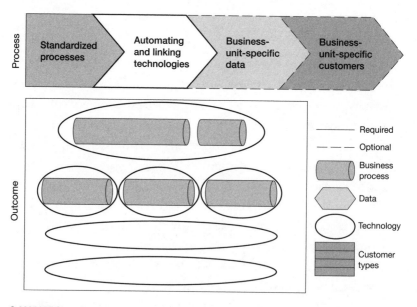

© 2005 MIT Sloan Center for Information Systems Research and IMD. Used with permission.

Who Should Design Enterprise Architecture?

In many companies enterprise architecture design is the responsibility of a small IT staff sequestered in a back room for several months, emerging only after drawing a book's worth of diagrams. These drawings often map out the linkages between existing systems. The exercise is justified by an expectation that mapping out existing legacy systems will lead to reduced complexity in the systems environment. Most of these architecture exercises end up abandoned on a shelf. Detailed architectural drawings of business processes and systems applications—apart from a specific business process initiative—can make companies feel as if someone is doing something about complexity, but they are rarely acted upon.

Instead, the enterprise architecture process should start with senior management debating the operating model. The templates for the core diagram for each operating model provide a starting point for helping management teams design their foundation for execution. In the process of populating an enterprise architecture core diagram, management must decide what is really core to the company. Choosing an operating model forces a decision on a general vision. Identifying the key customer types, core processes, shared data, and technologies to be standardized and integrated demands a commitment to a particular course of action. As a company builds the capabilities defined in the core diagram, implementing strategies around the core becomes easier, faster, and cheaper. However, once the core is in place, it is difficult to change the way the company does business. Not only must a company redesign and implement technical capabilities—its people must relearn processes. Thus, enterprise architecture embodies tough decisions by experienced managers. When it leads to process and system reuse, the benefits are enormous; when it forces standardization that doesn't fit business needs, it's very costly.

The idea that enterprise architecture discussions should involve senior management will not be a surprise to most IT executives. But many IT leaders find themselves taking the lead. We have seen two successful strategies to involve senior executives: IT-facilitated senior management discussions and senior management approval of IT-led designs.

IT Facilitates Senior Management Discussions

For some companies, enterprise architecture design efforts start with establishing core capabilities. Development of these capabilities will involve operational and often organizational reengineering. The scope of the changes is significant—and usually traumatic. These changes require senior management leadership, and start with mapping out the operating model and then the enterprise architecture core diagram. Companies using this approach include Delta Air Lines, BT, and State Street Corp. At BT and State Street, the CEOs announced transitions from Diversification models to more integrated models through initiatives they called "OneBT" and "One State Street" respectively.

Enterprise architecture core diagrams are tough to draw because they force management to develop a simple vision of a complex organization. Management is trying to articulate the essence of the company in the core diagram. Charlie Feld estimated that the management team at Delta Air Lines required sixty iterations to complete the drawing of its core diagram. But once complete, management should anticipate that, despite rapidly changing business conditions, the essence of the company will stay the same. The goal is to digitize the core to make it predictable, reusable, and reliable. By digitizing the core processes, data, and technologies depicted in the core diagram, management expects to provide a foundation for execution, not a set of handcuffs.

The inclination of some management teams is to include too many processes or too much detail in the enterprise architecture core diagram. Agreeing on what *not* to include can be a challenging but fruitful exercise in management focus. Intense management debate can expose options for the foundation for execution. The enterprise architecture design exercise forces clarification of a workable vision.

IT Leaders Design the Core Diagram

At MetLife business managers looked to the IT unit to provide systems rationalization as they drove benefits from prior and future acquisitions. The company lacked IT capabilities needed to elicit the value expected from its acquisitions. IT leaders developed the core diagram, offering a vision of the company that IT could start to deliver on quickly (figure 3-5). This core diagram envisioned significant business change, so senior managers needed to support and communicate the vision. Today, the integration hub has become a key capability in the company's operating vision. Fittingly, IT took the lead.

MetLife architects use their core diagram to communicate to senior managers and business partners the underlying logic for IT development. The core diagram shows how the architecture enables business objectives by providing a common customer view, improving information integrity, and reducing redundancy. It also guides the development of new applications by explaining how IT will deliver on the company's operating model.

Now What?

We have observed that some management teams can develop and share a clear vision without the benefit of core diagrams. But many management teams find a core diagram to be a helpful tool to create a shared understanding of how the company will function and then to communicate that shared vision to the rest of the organization. By thoughtfully preparing an enterprise architecture core diagram, management commits to IT and IT-enabled business processes that build and leverage a foundation for execution. Now comes the hard part—building and using it!

The building process is a journey. Companies learn from early initiatives how to build capabilities and how to get value from them. In the next chapter we describe this learning through four stages of enterprise architecture maturity.

4

Navigate the Stages of Enterprise Architecture Maturity

IN 1991 the city of Boston, Massachusetts, began a multiyear construction project to replace 7.8 miles of its elevated inner-city highway. Built in the 1950s, the old highway had long been a source of controversy. During the decade it was constructed, the old highway displaced 20,000 residents, cut off the North End and waterfront neighborhoods from Boston's economic hub, and blocked daylight and disrupted business. By the early nineties, the highway, which was designed to carry 75,000 vehicles per day, was experiencing near-constant congestion. Each day 200,000 vehicles crowded the highway, accidents happened four times more than the national average for urban interstates, and traffic was bumper-to-bumper for six to eight hours—and getting worse.[1]

Boston officials wanted a solution that not only handled greater numbers of vehicles but also eliminated an eyesore and enhanced the city's quality of life. The resulting vision was an underground highway system that would dismantle the elevated highway and allow development of parks and walkways to reunite the neighborhoods divided by the old highway. Unofficially dubbed the "Big Dig" (the official name was the Central Artery/ Tunnel Project), the project was intended to transform the highway system in Boston without crippling the city. Major components of the project included (1) building the widest cable-stayed hybrid bridge ever built and the first using an asymmetrical design; (2) creating a casting basin where sections of an underwater tunnel could be built and then floated out to the precise position where they would be lowered into the channel; and (3) applying a technique called "slurry walls," which reduced the area to be excavated in the building of the underground tunnels, thus minimizing disruptions to existing traffic.

Initial project estimates called for a budget of $2.6 billion and a completion date of 1998.[2] But the project was not completed until mid-2005 and cost nearly $15 billion. While many management decisions and some engineering mistakes contributed to the delays and cost overruns, the biggest factor was simple miscalculation. The Big Dig became the biggest public-works project in U.S. history. Key managers had underestimated the task involved in maintaining existing transportation capabilities while implementing a new infrastructure.

In building a foundation for execution, companies face some of the same challenges. New information technologies, changing industry boundaries, and the expanding global economy are creating new opportunities. But many of the processes and systems a company has built over time constitute obstacles to a new business vision. Management cannot shut down the company and start from scratch. Building a foundation for execution requires changing core processes and systems even as the company is depending on them to complete its daily operations. Management needs to redesign and then implement new systems, processes, and IT infrastructure without sabotaging daily operations.

Fortunately, unlike the Big Dig, firms navigate a fairly predictable path to achieve a foundation for business execution and follow a consistent pattern for building out their enterprise architectures.

We label this pattern the "four stages of architecture maturity."[3] The four stages are:

1. *Business Silos architecture:* where companies look to maximize individual business unit needs or functional needs

2. *Standardized Technology architecture:* providing IT efficiencies through technology standardization and, in most cases, increased centralization of technology management

3. *Optimized Core architecture:* which provides companywide data and process standardization as appropriate for the operating model

4. *Business Modularity architecture:* where companies manage and reuse loosely coupled IT-enabled business process components to preserve global standards while enabling local differences

Companies move through these stages by first building and then leveraging a foundation for execution. Each stage involves organizational learning about how to apply IT and business process discipline as strategic capabilities. Advancing through the stages requires lots of persistence, but as companies advance from the first stage to later stages, they realize benefits ranging from reduced IT operating costs to greater strategic agility. In this chapter we discuss how to navigate the enterprise architecture journey where companies learn to build and leverage their foundations for execution.

The Four Stages of Architecture Maturity

As companies build out their enterprise architecture, they gradually shift their investments in IT and business process redesign. In particular, they identify where global synergies offer greater value than local autonomy. Figure 4-1 shows the relative IT investments in data, shared infrastructure, enterprise systems, and local applications in each of the four architecture stages.

FIGURE 4-1

Architecture maturity stages

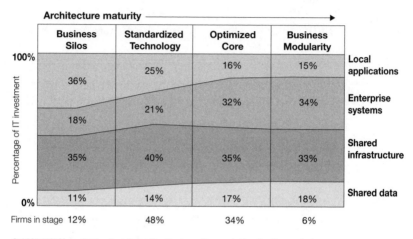

© 2005 MIT Sloan Center for Information Systems Research. Used with permission.

Stage 1: Business Silos

In the Business Silos stage, companies focus their IT investments on delivering solutions for local business problems and opportunities. These companies may take advantage of opportunities for shared infrastructure services like a data center, but such shared services accommodate the unique needs of the local business units. Companies in this stage do not rely on an established set of technology standards.

The role of IT in the Business Silos stage is to automate specific business processes. Thus, IT investments are usually justified on the basis of cost reductions. In a well-managed Business Silos environment, business managers design business processes and specify required IT functionality. IT then develops or buys an application to fully meet the requirements. Ideally, systems delivery in this stage generates a 100 percent solution to the specified business need.

Organizationally, applications in the Business Silos stage align naturally with a company's business unit, functional, or geographic structures. The architecture imposes no constraints on business units' activities, thereby encouraging innovation. Strategic initiatives can be executed with few, if any, constraints from other parts of the business. Consequently, functional, plant, and geographic managers often respond positively to applications developed in silos. Business silos can compete for capital funding using locally focused cost-benefit analysis. System benefits are predictable (albeit frequently overstated), and outcomes are measurable.

Solutions developed in a Business Silos architecture can enhance company competitiveness within the context of local specialization. For example, in an investment bank, IT is the product. New investment products are most profitable when they are first introduced (i.e., until competitors introduce a similar product). Thus, time to market is critically important in investment banking—each day a new product is on the market without a competing product can mean millions of dollars to the innovating company. Investment banks generate huge profits from these IT-based investment products.

These one-off solutions, however, create a legacy of systems that cannot talk to each other. Many IT professionals are quite adept at making disparate systems look integrated, but the code required to link applications becomes increasingly complex. Over time, key systems have so many links to other systems that even small changes are time consuming, expensive, and risky. More important, a Business Silos environment obstructs integration and standardization of business processes.

Only 12 percent of the companies in our research were in the Business Silos stage; most companies had already moved past this first architecture stage. It is not the frustration of isolated systems that usually drives management from this stage. It's the cost. More-lucrative industries, such as investment banking and pharmaceuticals, have thus been among the last to abandon the Business

Silos architecture. New, fast-growing businesses can easily fall into the trap of addressing immediate business needs without regard for future capabilities. Eventually, the need for efficiency in IT operations and the desire to build a solid data and process platform to support the business forces companies to move to the Standardized Technology stage.

Stage 2: Standardized Technology

In the Standardized Technology stage, companies shift some of their IT investments from local applications to shared infrastructure (figure 4-1). In this stage, companies establish technology standards intended to decrease the number of platforms they manage. Fewer platforms mean lower cost. In our study, Standardized Technology companies had IT budgets that were 15 percent lower than Business Silos companies.[4] But fewer platforms also mean fewer choices for IT solutions. Companies are increasingly willing to accept this trade-off. Forty-eight percent of companies in our study were in the Standardized Technology stage.

As in the Business Silos stage, the role of IT in the Standardized Technology stage is to automate local business processes. The emphasis in IT management, however, shifts from concerns about the functionality of the applications to the cost-effectiveness and reliability of the company's systems. Thus, the management of technology standards is key to this stage.

Early in this stage, most business unit managers and developers cling to the belief that business needs should drive technology. The initial encounter with technology standards is the first time management allows IT to shape business solutions. Soon business managers see that standardization reduces risk, and the costs of shared services (such as support, maintenance, and purchasing) and reliability, security, and development time improves. When these benefits become apparent—usually through benchmarking of IT unit costs and system quality—business unit managers quickly become believers. As one CIO noted: "We've had successes where we've been able to reduce people's costs by bringing in standard-ization. That has given us credibility. Their jaws hit the table when they saw the impact of standardization on their bottom line."

Most companies move into the Standardized Technology stage by creating a corporate CIO role or by endowing the incumbent CIO with authority to mandate IT-related behaviors. The CIO then introduces efficiencies by standardizing and consolidating technology platforms and providing shared infrastructure services. The migration to a Standardized Technology architecture fundamentally changes a company's approach to solutions delivery. Instead of defining the solution and looking for technology that best delivers that solution, companies in this stage negotiate the best possible solution given the acceptable technology platforms. The commitment to technical standards means that the IT application representing the best fit in terms of functionality may be rejected because it doesn't work with the company's technology architecture.

In addition to consolidating and standardizing hardware, companies in the standardized technology stage start to reduce the number of software products performing similar functions. For example, one manufacturer reduced the number of order management systems from twenty-eight to four—a common outcome of Standardized Technology initiatives. Technology standardization, however, does not readily overcome the Business Silos problem of data embedded in applications. Companies in this second stage usually increase access to shared data by introducing data warehouses, but transaction data is still embedded in individual applications.

Companies that have achieved significant cost savings and re-liability through Standardized Technology include Guardian Life Insurance, Johnson & Johnson, Carlson Companies, Brady Corp., and Pfizer. These organizations' managers found that early resistance to standards fades because after a while, early battles are forgotten and people stop questioning the value of standards or shared infrastructure. This evolution positions companies for the optimized core stage, where standardization practices expand to incorporate data and business processes.

Stage 3: Optimized Core

In the Optimized Core stage, companies move from a local view of data and applications to an enterprise view. IT staff eliminate data redundancy by extracting transaction data from individual applications and making it accessible to all appropriate processes. In this stage companies are also developing interfaces to critical corporate data and, if appropriate, standardizing business processes and IT applications. Thus, IT investments shift from local applications and shared infrastructure to enterprise systems and shared data (figure 4-1).

Thirty-four percent of companies in our study were in the optimized core stage. These companies are working to digitize their core data and/or business processes to capture the essence of their business. Companies choose to optimize their data, business process, or both depending on whether they're using a Diversification, Coordination, Replication, or Unification operating model. Once optimized and digitized, making fundamental changes to the business process or data becomes more difficult, but building new products and services onto the core becomes easier and faster.

The role of IT in the Optimized Core stage is to facilitate achievement of company objectives by building reusable data and business process platforms. Senior managers who lead the adoption of Optimized Core architectures embrace the principle that standardization enables innovation. In providing predictable business outcomes, standardized data and processes allow for process innovation closer to the customer.

Companies' reusable data and business process platforms are composed of a set of totally predictable core processes. Both at Air Products and Chemicals and at Nestlé, management is digitizing supply chains using ERP systems. UPS built its business around a single package database supporting its package delivery business.

Delta Air Lines created its Delta Nervous System to capture the interrelated requirements of the customer experience and airline operations. Citibank Asia Pacific established a core set of standardized banking processes that could be centrally served out of Singapore to both existing and new markets. In all of those cases, digitizing the company's core data and processes provided a foundation for existing and future operations and customer interactions. Each company's unique strategic advantage resulted from building on that foundation.

Optimizing the core processes and data in a company is a formidable technical challenge, but the corresponding management challenges are even more demanding. Standardizing shared data and core business processes involves taking control over business process design from local business unit leaders. Thus, the optimized core stage is a much harder sell to business managers than technology standardization. One CIO we interviewed described data and process standardization as "the most top-down effort we've ever made in this organization."

In the Optimized Core stage, senior IT and business managers learn together how to articulate the company's operating model and how to identify the IT capabilities required to implement the operating model. The architecture matures, enabling the company to optimize the core while identifying opportunities to leverage it. A more modular architecture is the next stage of maturity and business value.

Stage 4: Business Modularity

The Business Modularity architecture enables strategic agility through customized or reusable modules. These modules extend the essence of the business built into the infrastructure in the Optimized Core stage. Few companies have reached the Business Modularity stage—6 percent in our study—so it is difficult to assess how IT investment patterns change as companies move from the third to the fourth stage (figure 4-1).

In the fourth stage management refines, and increasingly modularizes, the processes that were digitized in the third stage. Management can take two approaches to this task. One is to create reusable modules and allow business units to select customer-oriented processes from a menu of options. For example, through a technology known as "Web services," companies can create reusable business services with standard interfaces for accessing those modules and the related data.[5] Web services can select modules from both internal and external sources. A second approach is to grant business unit managers greater discretion in the design of front-end processes, which they can individually build or buy as modules connecting to core data and back-end processes. In effect, managers get the freedom to bolt functionality onto the Optimized Core.

In either case, the role of IT in a Business Modularity architecture is to provide seamless linkages between business process modules. Modularity does not reduce the need for standardization. Individual process modules build on the standard core and link to other internal and external processes through standardized interfaces. To continue to provide all the benefits of the Optimized Core stage—efficiency, single face to the customer, process integration—modular architectures extend, rather than replace, Optimized Core architectures.

By ensuring the predictability of core processes, modular architectures provide a platform for innovation. The modular architecture enables local experiments, and the best ones can be spread throughout the company. To enable this, the Business Modularity stage requires negotiations between senior management and IT executives to clarify which processes are standardized, which are required, and which may be developed locally.

To benefit from modular architectures, companies must learn how to quickly identify the strategic opportunities that best leverage their core and then how to develop or reuse modules that extend the core. Reusable modules will build a thicker, denser core, providing greater efficiencies while allowing local customization. Quickly developed and very focused add-on modules allow strategic experiments that respond to changing market conditions. In the Business Modularity stage, companies reuse expertise in process, data, and technology standardization gained in earlier stages.

Organizational Learning: Key to Generating Value from Enterprise Architecture

As companies transition through the architecture stages, they fundamentally change how they do business. Companies in stage 1, which implement IT-enabled processes with little regard for business synergies with other processes, look nothing like companies in stage 4, where reusable business process modules have become a core discipline and the company has carefully delineated between enterprise and local processes and data. Getting from stage 1 to stage 4 is a journey. Some companies choose not to make that journey; others falter along the way. Understanding both the general nature of the organizational change at each stage and the specific learning enables companies both to generate value from the current stage and to prepare for the next.

Changing from a Local to a Companywide Perspective

As companies migrate through the architecture stages, they shift from a focus on local optimization to global optimization. This evolution has important implications for organizational flexibility. Most notably, through the second and third stages, companies are exchanging local flexibility for global flexibility. Figure 4-2 describes this change.

In the first stage, business unit managers have full control over their business and IT decisions. From an enterprisewide perspective, this limits global flexibility. For the company to introduce global change, all business unit managers first have to agree on the change, and then they need to simultaneously implement it. On the other hand, stage 1 companies can be highly responsive to local market changes because they are not constrained by global

FIGURE 4-2

Changes in organizational flexibility through the architecture stages

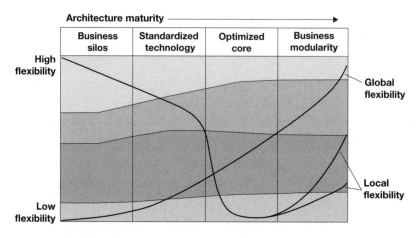

© 2005 IMD and MIT Sloan Center for Information Systems Research. Used with permission.

mandates. In addition, because they can—at least in theory—insist on the 100 percent solution to their business needs, they can design their business processes to their precise specifications and define IT requirements to support those processes.

In the standardized technology stage (stage 2), business units give up some discretion over technical decisions. Working within the constraints (and benefits) of technical standards, local business unit managers increasingly settle for the 80 percent solution, which reduces local flexibility. However, the use of standardized technologies increases global flexibility by reducing technical complexity and thus reducing implementation time.

Organizational change is felt most profoundly in the third stage. Optimized core means that local managers lose discretion over core business processes and sometimes over the people and systems that execute them. Companywide data and process standards disrupt local decision-making patterns. In some cases, standardized process designs (e.g., purchasing) introduce processes that are locally sub-optimal in favor of processes best suited to the company's global needs. But global flexibility increases as data becomes more trans-parent and processes become more comparable and predictable.

In the fourth stage, Business Modularity, flexibility grows both locally and globally. With a solid platform of core processes, data, and technology, a company can plug and play business modules on either level, and modular interfaces make changes simpler to implement. For example, ING DIRECT allows local managers to adjust what modules they use in response to local regulations and requirements, but the company expects its country-based man-agers to use standardized modules wherever possible to keep costs low. Executives can choose how much flexibility they want local managers to exercise. MeadWestvaco, as a paper manufacturer, fo-cuses on controlling cost. Building modules on its ERP system will give local managers greater autonomy over marketing decisions. Manufacturing decisions, on the other hand, will remain more standardized to maximize efficiencies.[6] The ability to customize global capabilities as appropriate is the benefit of the Business Modularity stage.

The shifting of flexibility between local and global manage-ment highlights the magnitude of change as companies move through the architecture maturity stages. In some cases, managers will resist these changes. In all cases, they will need to learn new behaviors. The time required to learn new behaviors means that the expected benefits of architecture maturity may be delayed. It is important that both IT and business managers recognize the need to allow time for learning. Otherwise, anxious managers may allocate large sums of money to technical upgrades, only to find that the organization is unable to absorb the capabilities the new technology makes available.

Because of the major organizational changes encountered at each new stage, we have found that companies cannot skip stages. We observed a number of unsuccessful attempts to skip stages—for example, a manufacturing company implementing an ERP system skipping from stage 1 to stage 3 and an investment bank implementing Web services skipping from stage 1 to stage 4. These companies invested significant resources in technologies intended to enable transformations. Management found, however, that the organizational changes exceeded the companies' capacity for change.[7] Following a major ERP implementation, one plant manager reported, "I feel like we turned out the lights but we keep trying to do our jobs anyway." Another stated, "It's like I'm standing on my head but still trying to manage." In several of the companies we spoke to, ERP implementations that tried to skip stages had to be halted or scaled back.

Learning How to Benefit from the Four Architecture Stages

Companies gradually learn to adapt to the changes demanded by each new stage. Through this learning process companies generate value from their current stage. Table 4-1 provides a summary of the changes associated with each new stage. Two characteristics define all four stages: (1) the IT capability being developed and (2) the strategic business implications of that capability. To support these evolving characteristics, companies must acquire learning in five areas:

1. Business objectives as captured in a formal business case (a document identifying expected costs and benefits)

2. Funding priorities, specifying the focus of major IT initiatives

3. Management capabilities key to generating benefits from new IT capabilities

4. Managers taking primary responsibility for defining applications

5. Critical IT governance issues

Successful organizational learning in each dimension results in greater business value and enhances the strategic importance of IT in the company. The bottom row of table 4-1 identifies the strategic implications of each stage.

TABLE 4-1

Learning requirements of the architecture stages

	Business Silos	Standardized Technology	Optimized Core	Business Modularity
IT capability	Local IT applications	Shared technical platforms	Companywide standardized processes or data	Plug-and-play business process modules
Business objectives	ROI of local business initiatives	Reduced IT costs	Cost and quality of business operations	Speed to market; strategic agility
Funding priorities	Individual applications	Shared infratructure services	Enterprise applications	Reusable business process components
Key management capability	Technology-enabled change management	Design and update of standards; funding shared services	Core enterprise process definition and measurement	Management of reusable business processes
Who defines applications	Local business leaders	IT and business unit leaders	Senior management and process leaders	IT, business, and industry leaders
Key IT governance issues	Measuring and communicating value	Establishing local/regional/ global responsibilities	Aligning project priorities with architecture objectives	Defining, sourcing, and funding business modules
Strategic implications	Local/functional optimization	IT efficiency	Business operational efficiency	Strategic agility

Source: Adapted from Jeanne W. Ross "Creating a Strategic IT Architecture Competency: Learning in Stages," *MIS Quarterly Executive* 2, no. 1 (March 2003): pp 31–43.

Business objectives for IT

In stage 1, companies usually create a business case for IT investments estimating the financial return on investment. Expected project outcomes tend to be localized and measurable. In stage 2, companies typically build their business case based on companywide IT cost reductions. As long as a company's IT unit costs are documented prior to standardization, the impact of new IT investments can be assessed. By stage 3, management has the more difficult challenge of measuring process improvements across functions or business units. The benefits may be difficult to trace to the bottom line, observable instead in increased customer satisfaction, reduced inefficiencies in the use of organizational resources, or more-efficient operations. In the fourth stage, the business case is based on metrics such as speed to market or strategic agility. Moving from stage 1 to stage 4 generally increases reuse of IT services (stage 2), data and processes (stage 3), and business modules (stage 4) with associated improvements in cost and speed to market. In the process of transitioning from one stage to the next, companies learn how to tackle these metrics.

Funding priorities

Consistent with business case changes, funding priorities change as companies move through the stages. These changes align with changes in their investment patterns discussed earlier in the chapter.

Key management capabilities

To generate value from IT investments, managers must lead the process changes enabled by new technology. If business processes don't change when new technology is installed, the investment has less value. As companies mature their architecture, management focus extends beyond local business process changes. Managers develop the capability to lead companywide change, first around technology standards and then around data and process standards. By the time the company reaches stage 4, the entire organization has become comfortable with the discipline of implementing, maintaining, and benefiting from standards. The company is ready to tackle the stage 4 challenge of building onto its standard platforms with internally and externally designed business process modules.

The transition from stage 1 to stage 2 introduces new levels of discipline in organizational process. This discipline starts slowly and focuses on IT management and use. The third stage greatly expands the need for discipline, and the fourth stage is dependent upon a culture of discipline. Organization members learn over time how to design, implement, and leverage standards. An individual can view any standard as an unnecessary constraint or as a simplifying mechanism. The individual's perception will be largely shaped by the extent to which a company has adopted a culture of discipline. A key component of this discipline includes aligned incentives (e.g., the right balance of companywide or local performance targets).

Who defines applications

In the first stage, local business managers usually define applications to support local business needs. By stage 2, IT leaders assume greater leadership across the company. Business leaders still establish requirements, but IT leaders define possible solutions and technology standards impose limits. In stage 3, the quest for enterprise solutions involves senior management and eventually high-level corporate process leaders. By the fourth stage, industry leaders are helping define applications by establishing industry standards while business and IT leaders negotiate solutions for their company. The change in who defines applications is reflected in implementation challenges. As business leaders lose tight control over applications requirements, it is more difficult for them to own business process changes.

IT governance

In stage 1, IT governance focuses on ensuring effective IT investments and accountability through careful business case development and effective project management. In the second stage, the company needs to set up effective governance mechanisms for implementing and maintaining technical standards. Stage 3 governance emphasizes the need to implement enterprise business objectives, and stage 4 demands governance of business process modules.

Learning Takes Time—Don't Skip Stages

Although companies can hire managers with experience in stage 3—and possibly even stage 4—companies cannot hire leadership that allows the company as a whole to skip a stage. Learning takes time. Companies differ in how long these transitions take, but for large companies each stage is several years. At Delta Air Lines and the government of the District of Columbia, the distinction between Standardized Technology and Optimized Core was blurred. Both organizations were in crisis when they started their architecture efforts. Delta was concerned about its ability to survive Y2K and the D.C. government was in bankruptcy. At Delta, management moved aggressively from Business Silos through Standardized Technology and into Optimized Core between 1997 and 2001. The D.C. government took six years (1999–2005) to make the same transition. These two organizations accelerated the Standardized Technology stage but allowed an extended period of time to develop their Optimized Core.

Changes are less disruptive at companies that pursue the stages one at a time. Guardian Life Insurance recognized significant cost-cutting benefits over a three-year Standardized Technology stage.[8] Guardian management focused on extracting maximum value from that stage before moving on to the next. Air Products and Chemicals also eased the shock of organizational change. While many companies in the oil and gas industry were attempting to skip from stage 1 to stage 3 by implementing ERP systems, Air Products instead worked deliberately through Standardized Technology before embarking on Optimized Core. The result was an easier transition from stage 2 to stage 3 and a single global implementation of its ERP system.[9]

Given the forces driving companies to optimize their cores, it can be difficult to work through the stages one by one. But it is our experience that there is no other way. Learning through the architecture stages encompasses both technology and business processes. On the technology side, companies learn how to invest their IT dollars for greatest impact, how to estimate the value of different IT investment opportunities, how to manage technology standards and secure compliance, and how to assess and communicate the value of IT. On the business process side, organizations learn how to design and manage enterprise processes, how to instill discipline in process execution, how to leverage IT capabilities in their business process initiatives, how to lead IT-enabled change, and how to define business process components. It is not enough for only senior managers to understand these concepts. Organizational learning must seep throughout a company for businesses to leverage IT and core business processes.

Building out an enterprise architecture is a long, challenging process. It involves ongoing negotiations about a company's business strategy and how IT both shapes and responds to that strategy. It also involves defining a target technology architecture (i.e., applications, data, and infrastructure technology) and doggedly pursuing that architecture even at times when immediate business needs beg for trade-offs.

How to Apply Architecture Maturity Stages in Your Company

As companies embark on their enterprise architecture journeys, they face their own Big Dig. Their challenge is to grow new business capabilities before dismantling the old. Like Boston's Big Dig—which separately opened a major tunnel, then a major bridge, then a major artery, and eventually a set of important interchanges—companies can generate significant benefits from incremental enhancements to their architecture. Unlike the Big Dig project, companies have the benefit of a road map derived from other successful companies making the same journey. As an added incentive, companies regularly generate benefits from small projects addressing a specific business need as they move toward an enterprise architecture and a platform for execution. For example, Guardian Life's CIO, Dennis Callahan, found that the company's IT unit costs started dropping early in its stage 2 efforts, and they kept dropping in subsequent years.

The objective of the enterprise architecture is not so much to achieve a particular end state as it is to recognize what direction the company is going. Transitioning through the architecture stages allows companies to rack up benefits. The four-stage model offers a number of lessons to companies attempting to generate more value from IT and implement greater process discipline:

- *Focus architecture efforts on strategic organizational processes.* Architecture exercises attempting to establish linkages between applications, data, and infrastructure for all of a company's business processes will almost certainly stall. No company can afford to eliminate all its silos. The best companies are focused on eliminating those silos that are limiting business efficiency and agility.

- *Move incrementally.* Skipping stages leads to either failures or delayed benefits. Companies will benefit more from small improvements in their existing stage than from higher-risk and premature moves into later stages.

- *Recognize that complex organizations have enterprise architectures at multiple levels.* Because architectures at different levels of the company support different business objectives, they can be at different maturity stages. Each stage requires its own set of management practices (see table 4-1), which should then be coordinated across the company.

- *Build an architecture capability in-house.* Inexperienced managers might want help, but negotiations leading to an understanding of business strategy and IT architecture require a close working relationship between business and IT. An ongoing dialogue about the relationship between IT and business process is essential for effective enterprise architecture. And, as we will discuss in chapter 7, you can outsource architectural initiatives, but you can't outsource architectural decision making.

- *Aim for business modularity.* Our research found that companies with more-mature architectures reported greater success in achieving strategic goals. And companies reporting greater success in achieving their strategic goals achieved higher average return on invested capital.[10] Companies with a Diversification operating model may have little need to advance beyond stage 1 or stage 2 (although even Diversification companies increasingly implement shared services that benefit from thinking about architecture maturity). All other companies will benefit from the flexibility that Business Modularity offers.

Companies reap a number of benefits from building out enterprise architecture. But the process of generating those benefits involves a great deal of learning—about the strategic direction of the company, about how IT contributes to that direction, and about how to manage IT and business process capabilities. In the next chapter we will discuss the benefits effective architecture can deliver at each stage as well as the management practices that help companies acquire and formalize the necessary learning.

5

Cash In on the Learning

WHEN LARGE NUMBERS OF BUSINESSES first installed electricity in their plants in the 1890s, they saw few immediate benefits. Electric generators replaced steam engines, but underlying business processes changed very little. Most factory engineers placed the new electrical generators in the same, central, cleverly architected position in the factory that enabled the steam engine to power as many machines as possible via mechanical driveshafts. It took decades for most factory engineers to redesign workflow and factory layout to take advantage of the increased flexibility and efficiency of electrical power. Not until forty years after the first central power station opened did electricity make a significant impact on business productivity.[1] The delay represented the learning required to take advantage of electrical capabilities.

In the auto industry, Henry Ford was the first to realize the potential of electric motors, and he used this knowledge to change forever the terms of competition in the industry.[2] Rather than power his factories with one or a few large engines, Ford used smaller electric motors to power each workstation, which allowed him to change the structure of his factory into an assembly line. As this new way of working was implemented, productivity increased, costs declined, and Ford steadily reduced the price of his cars. Sales took off—the first auto to be produced this way, the

Model T, saw sales grow from 6,000 in 1908 to 230,000 in 1914. As of 1919, half of all cars manufactured were produced using electrified manufacturing processes . . . all of them Fords.

Today's managers must redesign their companies as Ford did—this time, to take advantage of the potential of modern information technologies. Designing an enterprise architecture is the first step in building a foundation for execution capable of delivering the benefits of new technologies. But moving from architecture blueprint to realizing benefits requires managers to think differently about how business will be conducted.

In earlier chapters we have argued that to align IT with a company's strategic business initiatives, management must first define an operating model and then design and build out an enterprise architecture. So far, however, we have provided little evidence of the benefits of these efforts. In this chapter, we describe the evidence of the payoff from enterprise architecture. We've found that companies can start generating benefits soon after they commence the architecture maturity journey. These benefits grow as companies move into later architecture stages. We have also found that the goal is not to reach a particular endpoint. Companies learn, through their management practices, how to generate value from IT early in the journey. Those benefits multiply as long as the company continues to learn.

The Benefits of Enterprise Architecture

An enterprise architecture is critical for building a foundation for execution because it maps out important processes, data, and technology enabling desired levels of integration and standardization. In the process of implementing the enterprise architecture (i.e., building the foundation for execution), companies achieve a number of benefits, many of which can be tracked independently. Successful implementation of each stage of an enterprise architecture generates new or expanded technology and business benefits. These benefits are evident in five areas: IT costs, IT responsiveness, risk management, managerial satisfaction, and strategic business outcomes.

Reduced IT Costs

At most companies, concerns about IT costs drive the initial interest in enterprise architecture. In most cases, systems built to achieve immediate business needs have become expensive, redundant, and difficult to maintain. One financial services IT executive describes a familiar dilemma: "In the late 90s, accounts were growing exponentially . . . We had no time to look internally at rationalization or architecture. We grew our customer base through acquisition. We'd do the barebones, integrate the general ledger, make sure the networks could talk to each other and then move on to the next thing. In 2000 and beyond, market growth slowed down. All of a sudden, we're not acquiring, we're protecting current accounts. That's when we saw all these legacy problems, the problems of yesterday that we're dealing with today."[3]

As enterprise architecture introduces discipline in systems and processes, companies start to control the high costs of business silos. Companies can expect to reduce at least two types of IT costs:

- *IT operations unit costs:* the actual cost of services, such as laptop provision and support, the help desk, application operations, access to enterprise data, network capacity, and e-mail. Use of these services grows over time, but the unit costs should decrease with architecture maturity.

- *Applications maintenance costs:* the time and total cost for making changes to existing applications to reflect business and technology changes.

Figure 5-1 shows the magnitude of change in average IT costs as companies mature their enterprise architectures. The biggest

impact on cost is achieved in stage 2, as companies move to consolidate data centers, reduce the number of technologies in use,
and introduce standards to guide the platform design of new systems. On average, companies in stage 2 have 15 percent lower IT
budgets than companies in stage 1.[4] Global companies, and companies that have experienced repeated mergers, often cite much
higher savings. For example, at Celanese, a more than $5 billion
chemical company, standardizing technology addressed the negative IT cost impacts of several mergers and acquisitions. According to CIO Karl Wachs, "We went from a very diverse system and
process landscape to a pretty homogenous environment, and we
cut costs by 30 to 40 percent within four years. And, now, we deliver better services."[5]

FIGURE 5-1

Cost implications of architecture maturity

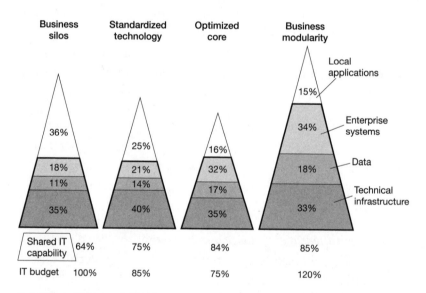

Note: IT budgets are corrected for industry differences. Application silo budget is the baseline. Budgets
for other stages are represented as a percentage of the baseline budget. Only five firms in stage 4
reported their IT budgets, so that data is not reliable.

As shown in figure 5-1, the main reason for the decrease in costs is that companies are investing in more shared (as opposed to business-unit-specific) capability. The shared IT capability—which includes technical infrastructure, shared data, and enterprise systems—increases from 64 percent to 75 percent of the company's IT investment between stage one and stage two.

The trend toward increased shared IT capability continues into the Optimized Core stage, growing to 84 percent of total IT investment. In the process, IT costs drop another 10 percent; IT budgets of stage 3 companies are 75 percent of stage 1 budgets. Even though companies typically make big investments in the third stage as part of business process integration and standardization efforts, their IT budgets, on average, decrease. The drop in local departmental or divisional spending offsets the increase in the central budget. Charlie Feld, former CIO at Delta Air Lines, explains the phenomenon this way: "Even though we spent hundreds of millions of dollars on the infrastructure . . . we were spending it anyway. That's the fallacy in what most people think. When it's being spent in departments and in divisions the money is being spent. It's just not being seen."[6]

By stage 4, even though companies are continuing to invest in shared IT capability, their IT costs rebound. IT budgets in stage 4 companies (for our small sample) are 20 percent higher than stage 1 budgets, an increase of 45 percent over stage 3 budgets. The increase in IT costs in the Business Modularity stage may result from several different factors. For example, costs that were previously hidden in business budgets may be converted to IT costs in stage 4 as business process modules are formed and true costs are allocated. In addition, early adopters of stage 4 architectures may experience higher costs associated with being on the leading edge. But the most important reason why Business Modularity may have higher costs is companies' increased investment in leading edge innovation.

Companies moving into Business Modularity have developed a solid foundation for execution. They have digitized their core business processes and have access to the critical customer and product data they need to develop new products and services. They start to see new opportunities to develop this core. These IT-enabled opportunities require IT investments, but the returns are easy to justify. These investments increase IT costs, but they also create new business opportunities.

Increased IT Responsiveness

In a standardized environment, IT and business leaders have fewer technology choices and thus spend less time making technology decisions or addressing unexpected technical problems. The result is reduced development time, including both the elapsed time and total development hours required to implement a new system. When companies are still relatively new, they can build silo applications rapidly, but as the silos multiply, those silos increasingly act as inhibitors to future development. In our research, IT executives noted a significant improvement in development time as a result of moving into stage 2 and working on more-standardized platforms.

The incremental improvement in IT responsiveness from moving to stage 3 is minimal. Many companies are implementing major enterprise systems in this stage. These projects are large and, for most companies, both IT and business expertise on these systems is limited. But IT responsiveness ratings climb dramatically as companies move into Business Modularity (average rating up 37 percent over stage 3). Whereas the third stage involves large-scale projects, stage 4 involves reusing or customizing smaller modules. By definition, faster development time should be a key benefit of achieving stage 4 architecture maturity. Figure 5-2 shows how CIOs rated the impact of architecture maturity on IT responsiveness and other benefits

Improved Risk Management

Cleaning up IT infrastructure, shared data, and enterprise applications provides a more manageable IT environment. This contributes to at least three risk-related benefits:

FIGURE 5-2

Benefits from increasing enterprise architecture maturity

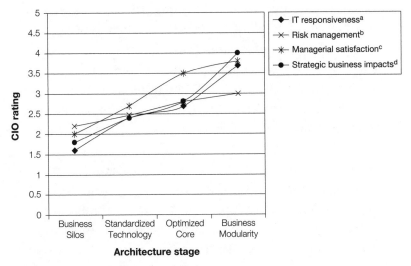

a. Development time
b. Business risk, security breaches, and disaster tolerance
c. Senior management and business unit management satisfaction
d. Operational excellence, customer intimacy, product leadership, and strategic agility

© 2005 MIT Sloan Center for Information Systems Research. Used with permission.

- *Reduced business risk:* the extent to which systems are consistently and reliably up and running as needed to support the business

- *Increased disaster tolerance:* the ability to minimize business losses during outages or natural disasters

- *Reduced security breaches:* avoidance of computer viruses and inappropriate access (both internal and external) to private or confidential data

While enterprise architecture demonstrates a positive impact on risk management, the impact is smaller than it is for the other benefits. However, in companies focused on building risk management into their enterprise architecture, the impact is much more dramatic. For example, PFPC, a subsidiary of PNC Financial

Services Group, provides a variety of financial services to corporate clients who demand a very high level of security and reliability. When Michael Harte became corporate CIO, he was expected to cut costs and improve service quality. He identified risk management as key to fulfilling his charge: "When I got here, I saw the need to position information technology as a business center that would enable the company to move from being focused on back office processing to being a leader in solution integration and information products. The first stage in that transformation was to bring greater discipline to risk management and governance as the foundation for change."[7]

PFPC's architecture efforts revolved around a Global Enterprise Platform initiative. Key efforts in this initiative reduced the number of technologies the company used, created a single portal for customer access to PFPC services, and restructured applications.

Early efforts on the Global Enterprise Platform initiative succeeded in taking PFPC through stage 2 of architecture maturity. IT spending decreased from 32 percent to 24 percent of total expenses. In addition, a U.S. Federal Reserve audit indicated that Harte had greatly improved PFPC's risk management competence. As the company now pursues business process and IT application improvements, Harte expects more risk management improvements.

Global events ranging from terrorists attacks to legislation like Sarbanes-Oxley will likely focus more attention on risk management as an outcome of enterprise architecture maturity. Companies with more-mature architectures are better positioned to meet these new demands for risk management.

Increased Management Satisfaction

Satisfaction is a more subjective measure, but it's important for generating enterprisewide commitment to architectural improvements and the organizational changes those improvements enable. Satisfaction scores indicate the confidence of non-IT executives in the IT unit's ability to deliver business value:

- Greater senior management satisfaction with IT reflects re-actions of corporate leaders.

- Greater business unit leader satisfaction with IT reflects attitudes of managers toward the impact of IT on local business results (e.g., costs, business value, service levels, reliability).

Satisfaction increases dramatically at each architecture stage. Despite the discomfort caused by major organizational change, senior managers clearly value the benefits. In advancing from stage 1 to stage 2, management sees the reductions in IT costs—invariably accompanied by increased IT responsiveness and improved IT services. From stage 2 to stage 3, senior managers become more involved in aligning IT with the strategic direction of the company. Jim Barrington, CIO of Novartis, a $28 billion pharmaceutical company, describes how the conversation about IT changes:

> I really to want to find out what [business managers'] real business issues are—what works well in the business, what doesn't work well in the business. And, then, perhaps try to figure out from an IT perspective how we can address some of those areas, particularly the ones that don't work well, or to understand their top three strategic drivers, let's say. In consumer health, it's customer excellence. So, I want to know all about customer excellence so that we can direct some of our IT resources to see what it means for us. Does it mean technology? Does it mean more understanding of process? Does it mean bringing systems from multiple business units together? What information do they need to drive the business?[8]

Management satisfaction increases again in stage 4. Ideally, by stage 4, the distinction between IT and business disappears.

Enhanced Strategic Business Outcomes

While all the benefits identified thus far can have bottom-line impacts, the most compelling need for enterprise architecture is to enable strategic business goals. Companies derive four important strategic outcomes from enterprise architecture:

1. *Better operational excellence:* low-cost, reliable, and predictable operations, with an emphasis on cost

2. *More customer intimacy:* extraordinary customer service, responsiveness, and relationships, based on deep customer knowledge

3. *Greater product leadership:* first to market with innovative products and services, usually dependent on rapid R&D to develop and commercialize

4. *More strategic agility:* the ability to respond rapidly to competitor initiatives and new market opportunities[9]

Strategic business outcomes increase dramatically from the first to the second and the third to the fourth stages of architecture maturity. The lesser impact of the transition to stage 3 is likely related to the scope of the organizational change. Managers at companies like Dow Corning, for example, have noted that major enterprise systems cause significant discomfort before they start delivering measurable business and IT benefits.[10]

The payback for higher IT expenses in stage 4 is evident in the strategic impact of enterprise architecture initiatives. Overall, executives rated strategic business benefits 40 percent higher in stage 4 than in stage 3. These benefits come from having a set of well-engineered business modules that provide a platform for execution and agility at a more granular level than that of stage 3. For example, Citibank Asia Pacific developed a new credit-card-processing module yielding a 50 percent reduction in processing costs. The company then reused this module to quickly enter new markets in Asia and Eastern Europe. Chapter 8 provides detailed examples of how UPS, 7-Eleven Japan, MetLife, and CEMEX have reaped strategic benefits from enterprise architecture maturity.

Management Practices for Realizing Value from Architecture Maturity

Generating the expected benefits of a foundation for execution results not just from changing IT investment patterns (as described in chapter 4), but also from new management practices. These new management practices formalize organizational learning about how to leverage IT capabilities and adopt business process changes. Practices include both formal roles (e.g., project architects, enterprise process owners, steering committees) and managerial processes (e.g., architecture exception processes, postimplementation reviews, business case development).

Many architecture practices are widely deployed, but the impact of each practice varies with how effectively a company has implemented it (figure 5-3). For example, less than 70 percent of companies have created full-time enterprise architecture teams, but those that have rate the teams as highly valuable. In contrast, a similar number of companies have implemented an architecture exception process, but they find that this practice is considerably less effective in generating business value.

Different stages place different demands on management, so some management practices are important for capturing the benefits of early stages while other practices are less important—and sometimes unnecessary—until later stages. Figure 5-4 shows the stage at which key management practices become important. The need for growing numbers of management practices reflects that increased learning is important to first building and then generating value from a foundation for execution. As a company implements each practice in figure 5-4, organizational learning accumulates for future organizational change processes.

FIGURE 5-3

Enterprise architecture management practices

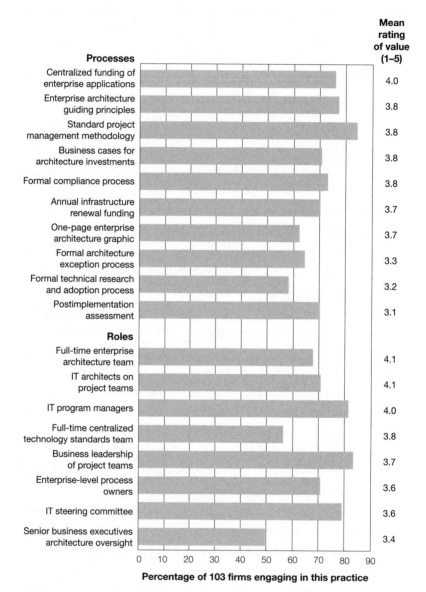

Note: Ratings represent the value received from these practices as reported by 103 CIOs.

© 2005 MIT Sloan Center for Information Systems Research. Used with permission.

FIGURE 5-4

How architecture management practices evolve

Business Silos	Standardized Technology	Optimized Core	Business Modularity
Business cases ⟶			
Project methodology ⟶			
	Architects on project teams ⟶		
	IT steering committee ⟶		
	Architecture exception process* ⟶		
	Formal compliance process* ⟶		
	Infrastructure renewal process* ⟶		
	Centralized funding of enterprise applications* ⟶		
	Centralized standards team ⟶		
		Process owners* ⟶	
		Enterprise architecture guiding principles* ⟶	
		Business leadership of project teams* ⟶	
		Senior executive oversight* ⟶	
		IT program managers* ⟶	
			Enterprise architecture core diagram*
			Postimplementation assessment*
			Technology research and adoption process*
			Full-time enterprise architecture team
Architecture maturity ⟶			

* These items are statistically significant related to architecture maturity; they are associated with greater value in later stages. We identified the stage at which each practice emerged as most important by comparing the means and determining the stage at which the value of the practice demonstrated its largest increase in mean value.

© 2005 MIT Sloan Center for Information Systems Research. Used with permission.

Stage 1 Management Practices

In our research only two practices proved critical for supporting companies' efforts to generate value from the Business Silos stage:

1. *Business cases:* accurate and compelling analyses of the expected costs and benefits of a proposed change to a business process or technology

2. *Standardized project methodology:* a disciplined, consistent approach to converting an approved project concept into an improved business process

This finding suggests that no IT governance or organizational change processes are necessary in the first stage. When a business unit owns its IT projects, good leaders see to it that the project generates value. Getting business cases and project methodology right doesn't sound very hard—but for most companies, it takes lots of practice!

It is unwise to move into the second stage of architecture maturity before these two management practices have become part of the company's DNA. These first two practices help companies generate value in the first stage, but the value these practices generate actually increases as companies mature their architectures. Companies with weak business case and project methodology practices will need to acquire those management practices while simultaneously attempting to develop practices specific to later stages.

Stage 2 Management Practices

Stage 2 presents companies with far more daunting management challenges. As they standardize technology, companies force new behaviors on their business unit leaders and IT developers. When it comes to IT decisions, these leaders need to start thinking about what's best for the company in addition to the business units' needs. This change in thinking affects how companies fund IT and initiatives to change business processes as well as how they manage the standardized technologies they are introducing.

Three critical management practices in stage 2 address issues related to more centralized IT funding:

1. *An IT steering committee:* a small group of executives held accountable for determining IT priorities

2. *Centralized funding of enterprise applications:* capital budget allocations supporting implementation of enterprisewide standards

3. *An infrastructure renewal process:* a funding mechanism for projects intended primarily to retire aging technologies and upgrade the technology base

Four other practices relate to managing a standardized technology environment:

1. *A formal architecture compliance process:* a process for ensuring new projects are adopting standard technologies

2. *Architects on project teams:* individuals responsible for ensuring that technical standards are observed or that necessary exceptions are adopted

3. *An architecture exception process:* a formal process for identifying when exceptions to standards add value

4. *A centralized standards team:* technical experts who identify appropriate standards and recognize when to retire or update those standards

The seven practices important to stage 2 reflect the growing need to address the challenges of using IT as a companywide, rather than business unit or functional, asset. Combined, they represent a significant difference in managing a stage 2 environment relative to a stage 1. For example, in 1996 a $5 billion process manufacturer learned that the company's IT spending represented 3.6 percent of sales compared to an industry average of 2 percent. To bring IT costs under control, management supported a transition to Standardized Technology. The CIO noted that this decision led to a number of important changes: "So, over the ensuing five years we repatriated all of the IT from the groups and the geographies—that all reports centrally now. We standardized the desktop; we standardized the service offerings and our approach to services, which changed the budgeting mechanisms and governance mechanisms to focus on fewer higher-impact things rather than the literally thousands of small projects that were getting done."

As a result of initiating all seven of the recommended practices for stage 2, management had developed habits easing the transition into the Optimized Core. In 2001, with its IT costs around industry average, the company began an ERP implementation. By 2004 management declared that key business processes were globally standard and efforts to transform the company had resulted in an 18 percent increase in revenues and a 52 percent increase in operating income over the prior year.

Stage 3 Management Practices

The practices implemented in stage 2 are not sufficient to help companies succeed in stage 3. Rebecca Rhoads is vice president and CIO at Raytheon, a $21 billion aerospace and defense company that has grown to its current form through mergers with Texas Instruments, Hughes, General Dynamics, and E-Systems. She explains that the practices guiding Raytheon to Standardized Technology following the mergers were just the first step in learning how to generate value from IT:

> Over time, you will outgrow the governance model that makes you successful. And it took me awhile to figure that out because we had developed a governance model that was so effective—everybody was so supportive of it. We had buy-in and alignment, and it was a governance

model that helped us consolidate and shape the company. So once we reduced a couple thousand legacy applications, once we went from 150 payroll systems to one, 28 email systems to one, we reduced IT spend by over 40 percent. That's what we needed to do over the first three to four years of being the new company, because if you don't get the synergy of the merger in that timeframe, you're not going to ever be able to come up for air.[11]

Stage 3 management practices help companies to understand the need for process integration and standardization and to adjust to the resulting organizational changes. Process standardization depends on senior management leadership. Five practices emerging as important in stage 3 include:

1. *Enterprisewide process owners:* individuals who own, design, and implement one or more enterprisewide processes

2. *A statement of enterprise architecture guiding principles:* tough choices specifying how IT will be applied in the company (e.g., to serve customer interests versus to cut business process costs)

3. *Business leadership of project teams:* high-level managers accountable for generating expected benefits and actively involved in project management

4. *Senior executive oversight of enterprise architecture:* high-level reviews of enterprise architecture initiatives and design of incentives to encourage adoption

5. *IT program managers:* individuals who coordinate systems and projects to map integration and minimize redundancy

Rhoads found that, following the cost-cutting success, Raytheon's senior management team started to adopt practices articulating business direction and defining companywide processes.

At Raytheon, Rhoads says, these practices focused on how the company would grow:

> We had fine-tuned a governance model, a financial model, planning tools, everything around consolidating legacy systems *and* reducing our spend. We were successful in pulling down and getting the right systems in place for the company to manage human capital and finances. What we found next was that very quickly, once we had kind of declared victory around that, the shoe was too small—the governance model didn't fit right anymore. When we looked at our growth strategy and the fact that we had to start making some important investments, and maybe even some aggressive investments, the governance model didn't support that.[12]

As the name implies, the Optimized Core stage involves digitizing key business processes into the foundation for execution. The critical management practices in stage 3 ensure that senior management is defining what processes are built into the foundation and providing ongoing leadership to protect and enhance the capabilities constituting the foundation.

Stage 4 Management Practices

Companies in the fourth stage are sophisticated users of IT. They have developed disciplined business processes and are learning how to define standard process components, enabling greater agility in response to different business opportunities and customer needs. The critical management practices in this stage focus on how companies communicate architecture goals and assess their IT-enabled business change initiatives. Four practices are key to stage 4:

1. *A one-page core diagram:* a tool that communicates a high-level picture of integration and standardization requirements (as described in chapter 3)

2. *Postimplementation assessment:* a formal process for securing and communicating lessons learned from each project

3. *A formal research and adoption process:* a process for identifying the new technologies that could have a significant impact on the company

4. *A full-time enterprise architecture team:* IT staff who help fit immediate business needs into the company's longer-term vision

These practices accelerate learning about the role of IT in enabling the business. BT, formerly British Telecom, is a £18.6 billion U.K. company in the midst of transforming from a telephone company to a provider of telecommunications solutions. To support the transformation, BT is aggressively pursuing the benefits associated with accelerated learning by instituting ninety-day project cycles. Al-Noor Ramji, Group CIO of BT, describes the company's review process at the end of each cycle: "Every ninety days, every IT program undergoes a postimplementation review, or PIR. We use PIRs to make sure every program is delivering on its commitments; if they don't deliver, the PIR process will cut them off. The important thing is to measure and then calibrate all the programs every ninety days. It's a new way of working, but after a few cycles, people get used to it."[13]

As Ramji notes, people get used to this kind of learning. In fact, by stage 4, companies have learned how to squeeze additional benefits from practices instituted in stage 1. For example, postimplementation reviews inform the business case by providing evidence of the actual benefits received from earlier projects. Consequently, the estimated benefits for proposed projects become more predictable and realistic as companies move through the architecture maturity stages.

Lessons from Top Performers: What Helps the Most?

Large companies reaping benefits from stage 4 architectures have generally implemented most, if not all, of the practices in figure 5-4. All of these practices can make enterprise architecture efforts more valuable, but they are not equally important. Specifically, top performers distinguish themselves from other companies in three ways: greater senior management involvement in enterprise architecture issues; greater effort to build architecture into project methodology; and more mature enterprise architecture (table 5-1).

TABLE 5-1

Lessons from high-performing companies

Characteristic	Low strategic effectiveness (n = 78 firms)	High strategic effectiveness (n = 25 firms)
Senior management involvement		
Senior management explicitly defined architecture requirements	25% (of firms)	44% (of firms)
Senior management oversees architecture initiatives	45% (of firms)	60% (of firms)
Senior managers who can describe high-level architecture	19% (of managers)	39% (of managers)
Architecture built into project methodology		
Project teams with architects assigned	49% (of projects)	81% (of projects)
Projects subject to architecture compliance review	60% (of projects)	80% (of projects)
Median architecture maturity stage (1–4)	2	3

Note: Statistically significant difference between the responses of top 25% of firms on strategic effectiveness. Strategic effectiveness is measured as strategic outcomes (operational excellence, customer intimacy, product innovation, and strategic agility) of architecture initiatives weighted by their relative importance to each firm. The top 25% of firms on strategic effectiveness reported significantly higher profitability, which correlated with industry-adjusted measures of companywide profitability.

Greater Senior Management Involvement

High performers on strategic effectiveness enjoy greater senior management involvement in enterprise architecture planning and implementation. For example, senior management teams explicitly define the requirements for enterprise architecture at almost half of the top-performing companies, but at only one-quarter of the other companies. And senior management involvement does not stop at the planning stage. Senior managers in high performers are also more than twice as likely as their counterparts in other firms to be able to describe their company's enterprise architecture. They also provide oversight on architecture initiatives.

In big companies, it's easy to imagine overwhelming senior managers and everyone else with IT and business process issues. Ramji explains how BT brought its priorities into focus:

> When I arrived at BT, there were 4,300 active projects. The average person was working on 5.3 projects at any given time. To introduce greater discipline and focus, we developed an ROI model and pushed everything through it; as a result, we now have under 30 programs . . . and the programs are judged on ROI. If there's no ROI because it's a speculative program, CEO sign-off is required. Now, that's discipline, and it frames the discussion around the right issues. Why would we do this without an ROI or a CEO signature? We shouldn't do it just because someone dreamt it up.[14]

Like many companies with more-mature architectures, BT has reduced the number of projects it pursues at one time. Otherwise, management attention can be diluted on projects of little significance to the company. The increased focus afforded by fewer initiatives improves outcomes on the projects that matter most.

Architecture Built into Project Methodology

Companies realizing strategic benefits from enterprise architecture have project methodologies emphasizing the importance of architecture. Successful companies involve IT architects early in project design and typically demand that projects pass an architectural compliance review. In these companies the IT architect plays a pivotal role in project implementation.

For example, at one financial services firm, an IT architect is assigned to every project. The architect reviews requirements and identifies any needed capabilities that are inconsistent with architecture standards. The architect is authorized to take actions in the company's best interest—which may involve forcing a compromise on functionality to maintain architectural integrity or, conversely, allowing an exception to the standards to meet a unique business need. As in many companies that have established a key role for IT architects on business projects, the architects in this company play the additional role of jointly establishing architecture standards. This means identifying when standard technologies are outdated. It also means identifying the need for new infrastructure capabilities and defining a standard before a new project chooses one by default. Recently, this financial services company defined a standard for an integrated voice response system in anticipation of several upcoming initiatives that otherwise would have sought their own solutions.

Greater Architecture Maturity

As companies mature their architectures, they position themselves for greater strategic impact from IT because their focus shifts from technology standardization to IT-enabled process standardization and integration. Maturing involves transitioning from systems and platforms that resemble a plate of cold spaghetti to modular architectures suited to a plug-and-play business model. Companies generate benefits in every stage, but they don't acquire strategic business benefits until later stages. Not surprisingly, then, top-performing companies have more-mature architectures.

The Evolving Role of the CIO

The CIO is a key driver—in most companies, the CIO is *the* key driver—of enterprise architecture benefits. As companies advance through the architecture stages, they need different CIO skills and governance models. Brent Glendening is the CIO of the elevators and escalators division of Schindler, an SFr 8.3 billion (approximately $6.3 billion) manufacturer located in Ebikon, Switzerland. He has led his company from Business Silos through Standardized Technology into Optimized Core, and is now moving it into Business Modularity.[15] He is one of the few CIOs in our research who has led his company through more than one transformation. He describes his role in migrating from stage 1 to stage 2 as having a technical focus: "Back in the early 1990s the CIO role was very technical. Both my country IT managers and myself had to understand the technology, keep it running, and manage the vertical projects under our control. We saw that hardware standardization was a critical success factor for the tasks at hand and was a prerequisite for moving to an optimized core."

Glendening led the introduction of a number of critical stage 2 management practices:

> The challenge was to choose the right platforms and enforce the standards. Coordination with finance and purchasing was critical to ensure that the benefits of a standardized environment were not eroded by rogue purchases. Enforcing and deploying the standards also provided us with the opportunity to set up IT steering committees in each country to explain and enforce IT decisions. The IT steering committees consisted of the country president, key business owners, and the country IT managers. As standards were deployed, these committees evolved from enforcement to the

establishment of IT strategy and the prioritization of projects and resources.

By the late nineties, Glendening was helping the business assess the need for a transition to stage 3:

> The move to standardized processes was three to four times more difficult than the move to standardized hardware. There were three stages of learning we had to take the country presidents through. The first was, "Will it work?" Will a standard process be able to fully support the needs of my country? The next stage was, "What does it mean for my business?" How will the structure, roles, and performance of my business unit change? Then, finally, "What does it mean for me?" How would the job of a country president change? Only after answering all of these questions would they trust us enough to jointly redesign their entire business processes, based on uniform corporate products and processes.

Glendening found he had to transform his own skills, as he attempted to guide the business transformation: "To make the leap to standardized processes, you must earn the trust of the business unit presidents and key executives. That will only happen if you understand how the business works and can talk about the business in their language. You have to be a businessman first and a technologist second."

Glendening's experience is representative of other CIOs we surveyed. Each transformation required new leadership skills, as summarized in table 5-2. We also found that as these skills evolved, the titles of the CIOs we surveyed evolved as well. In the companies in the Business Silos stage, the head of IT had only the CIO or vice president of IT title. Of the companies in the Standardized Technology stage, 36 percent of the CIOs had a second, business-oriented title such as vice president of strategy or vice president of logistics. Of the companies in Optimized Core or Business Mod-

ularity, 50 percent of the CIOs had these second titles. This evolution of titles is a signal to the organization about the skills, knowledge, and responsibilities of the CIO.

There is no reason that one person, or a top team of two or three
leaders, cannot have all the skills listed in table 5-2 and provide
the leadership needed to move the company through multiple
phases. But hiring the right CIO requires that companies understand where they are going in the longer term with their operating
model and architecture. More top-level support should strengthen
the recent trend of longer tenures for CIOs.

TABLE 5-2

As the company's architecture matures, the CIO role evolves

	Business Silos	Standardized Technology	Optimized Core/ Business Modularity
Key skills of the CIO	• Technical knowledge to help with standards decisions • Ability to implement standard project methodology and oversight • Ability to work with top management team to establish basic governance • Ability to make business case for standardization	• Detailed knowledge of how the business functions • Ability to manage large organizational change efforts • Credibility with business unit or functional heads • Ability to manage large central budget • Understanding of architecture as a business enabler	• Ability to facilitate innovation off new platform • Detailed knowledge of core business—could potentially run a business unit if necessary • Ability to delegate ownership of key process and data modules while still ensuring adherence to standards • Understanding of strategic benefits of architecture
Reports to:	CEO or CFO	CEO	CEO
Percentage of IT heads with second title*	0%	26%	50%

*Percentage of CIOs having second VP title, from samples of 25 CIOs in the United States and Europe.

© 2005 IMD. Used with permission.

6

Build the Foundation
One Project at a Time

SEVERAL YEARS AGO a friend of ours invited an interior decorator to refurbish the living room in her family's house. The decorator pointed out that any change to the living room would force
changes in the adjoining dining room if the home was to look
"put together." No problem. But the eventual theme of the living room and dining room argued for redoing the stairs to the second floor. Of course, the carpet on the stairs extended throughout
the second floor (and quantity discounts were available), so the
carpet in the entire house was slated for replacement. Unfortunately, the temptation to choose new and exciting colors for the
carpet proved too much to resist. But that meant the new carpet
wouldn't match the existing walls or draperies. Ultimately, the family had to move out of the house for six weeks so the decorator
could fulfill her vision. The final effect was, to be sure, magnifi-
cent. And expensive.*

Companies encounter similar temptations when they map out
their foundation for execution. Once a vision is clear, it seems

---

*This chapter was coauthored with Nils O. Fonstad, a research scientist at
the MIT Sloan Center for Information Systems Research.

logical that the fastest way to create the foundation is to tear out existing—typically functional—processes and systems. In times of crisis or disruptive change, massive projects that build a new foundation can make sense. A company may need to transform quickly to survive. But massive change is expensive and risky, sometimes *too* expensive and risky for a company to pursue all at once.

Large systems-based implementations have a lousy track record of success. Many companies have implemented extensive ERP systems, expecting their core business processes to be automated into a foundation. The size, complexity, disruption, cost, and learning required all contributed to the failure of more than 50 percent of these implementations, with millions of dollars and much management goodwill going down the drain.[1]

The alternative to the "big-bang" implementations is to build the foundation one project at a time. To do so, every business project must not only meet its short-term business goals but also help implement (or at least not undermine) the company's architecture. Assigning each project responsibility for implementing a piece of the architecture has at least three benefits. First, it ensures that the architecture isn't an ivory-tower abstraction of the world, but a useful model for how to do business. Second, it ensures that the foundation for execution becomes increasingly robust as the business and available technology evolve. Finally, it can cut costs dramatically by distributing the costs and risks of implementing the company's enterprise architecture across many smaller and more-manageable projects. It is often no more expensive to implement project solutions in an architecturally sound manner, and over time the progress toward implementing the company's desired architecture is substantial.

The IT Engagement Model

Building a foundation one project at a time requires the engagement of key stakeholders in the design, implementation, and use of new IT and business process capabilities—an IT engagement model. We define the *IT engagement model* as the system of governance mechanisms assuring that business and IT projects achieve both local and company-wide objectives.[2] At top performing companies the engagement model has three main ingredients:

1. *Companywide IT governance:* decision rights and accountability framework to encourage desirable behavior in the use of IT

2. *Project management:* formalized project methodology, with clear deliverables and regular checkpoints

3. *Linking mechanisms:* processes and decision-making bodies that align incentives and connect the project-level activities to the overall IT governance

In large companies, the IT engagement model contains six key stakeholder groups: the overall company management, business unit management, and line or project management—each of which exists on both the IT and business sides of the company. (See figure 6-1.) The different perspectives, objectives, and incentives of these groups create two challenges: coordination and alignment.

At the company level, senior leaders set direction, create a climate for success, and design incentives to meet companywide goals. Business unit leaders focus on the performance of their business unit. Project leaders are typically entirely focused on the success of their projects, garnering all the company resources they can find, beg, borrow, or steal to get the job done.

The IT engagement model *coordinates* these three different levels: company, business unit, and project. The IT governance establishes high-level goals and incentives. Project management applies the best practices of company-specific project management tools and techniques to every major project, ensuring local project success. Linking mechanisms ensure that, as projects move forward, they reflect and inform the goals and priorities of all parties.

The second challenge of engagement is to *align* the company's IT and business activities to ensure that value is generated from IT investments. In some top-performing companies, IT-business alignment is ingrained in every management process. More often,

FIGURE 6-1

The IT engagement model

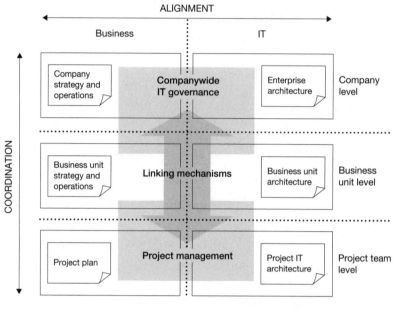

© 2006 MIT Sloan Center for Information Systems Research and IMD. Used with permission.

however, the IT and business managers' conflicting priorities lead to unresolved differences. IT executives focus on providing the most powerful, risk-free IT environment possible. Business leaders focus on cutting costs and delivering rapid solutions. Constructive tension between business and IT leads to effective resolution of these discrepancies. The IT engagement model helps leaders recognize and resolve their differences in accordance with companywide business objectives.

By linking IT governance and project management, the engagement model coordinates and aligns. Without an engagement model, project leaders execute in isolation. They choose solutions that meet project goals, but the company's overall goals for integration and standardization are ignored and the foundation for execution never emerges. In this chapter we further describe the ingredients of the IT engagement model and give examples of each. We then show all three in action using a case example.

IT Governance

IT governance is the decision rights and accountability framework for encouraging desirable behaviors in the use of IT. IT governance reflects broader corporate governance principles while focusing on the management and use of IT to achieve corporate performance goals.[3] IT governance shouldn't be considered in isolation because IT is linked to other key company assets (i.e., financial, human, know-how/intellectual property, physical, and relational assets). Thus, IT governance might share mechanisms, such as executive committees and budget processes, with other asset-governance processes, thereby aligning companywide decision-making processes.

IT governance encompasses five major decision areas related to the management and use of IT in a firm, all of which should be driven by the operating model:

1. *IT principles:* high-level decisions about the strategic role of IT in the business

2. *Enterprise architecture:* the organizing logic for business processes and IT infrastructure

3. *IT infrastructure:* centrally coordinated, shared IT services providing part of the foundation for execution

4. *Business application needs:* business requirements for purchased or internally developed IT applications that both use and build the foundation for execution

5. *Prioritization and investment:* decisions about how much and where to invest in IT, including project approval and justification techniques

Each of these decisions can be made by corporate, business unit, or functional managers—or some combination—with the operating model as a guide. Thus, the first step in designing IT governance is to determine who should make, and be held accountable for, each decision area. To help think about who should make these decisions, we provide in table 6-1 a sample of the questions that each decision area should cover.

Every company engages in IT decision making, but firms differ considerably in how thoughtfully they have defined *accountability* and how rigorously they formalize and communicate decision-making processes. Without formal IT governance, individual managers are left to resolve isolated issues as they arise. These individual actions can be at odds with each other and can lead to misalignment and a lack of coordination. For example, the CIO at a global transportation firm was instructed to cut the corporate IT budget. This CIO introduced a charge-back system to curtail demand for IT services. Unhappy with the new charges, managers within each of the business units hired local technical specialists to provide services. The new technical specialists did not show up in the corporate IT budget, so it looked as if the CIO had achieved his goal, but the new business unit hires increased, rather than decreased, the firm's total IT spending. Worse, the business unit employees developed local services that compromised the integrity of the company's architecture, reducing the quality of service for customers of more than one business unit.

In contrast, when UNICEF's senior managers recognized that IT was playing an increasingly strategic (and expensive) role in enabling the organization's mission of delivering services to children, the senior management team defined the role of IT in the organization, decided on project priorities and funding levels, clarified the need for shared services, and established organizationwide standardization and integration requirements.[4] These managers held division directors accountable for implementation of global systems, and the CIO was held accountable for delivering key infrastructure services and coordinating IT use for the company.

TABLE 6-1

Key issues for each IT decision

IT principles	• How does the operating model translate to IT principles to guide IT decision making?
	• What is the role of IT in the operating model?
	• What are IT-desirable behaviors?
	• How will IT be funded—by the company or by business units?
Enterprise architecture	• What are the company's core business processes? How are they related?
	• What information drives these core processes? How must this information be integrated?
	• What technical capabilities should be standardized companywide to support IT efficiencies and facilitate process standardization and integration?
	• What activities must be standardized companywide to support data integration?
	• What technology choices will guide the company's approach to IT initiatives?
IT infrastructure	• What infrastructure services are most critical to achieving the company's operating model?
	• What infrastructure services should be implemented companywide?
	• What are the service-level requirements of those services?
	• How should infrastructure services be priced?
	• What is the plan for keeping underlying technologies up to date?
	• What infrastructure services should be outsourced?
Business application needs	• What are the market and business process opportunities for new business applications?
	• How can business needs be addressed within architectural standards?
	• When does a business need justify an exception to the standards?
	• Who will own the outcomes of each project and institute organizational changes to ensure value?
	• What strategic experiments should we take on? How should we measure success?
IT investment and prioritization	• What process changes or enhancements are strategically most important to the company?
	• What is the distribution in the current IT portfolio? Is this portfolio consistent with the company's objectives?
	• What is the relative importance of companywide versus business unit investments? Do actual investment practices reflect their relative importance?
	• What is the right balance between top-down and bottom-up projects to balance standardization and innovation?

Over the past few years, IT has fundamentally transformed the way UNICEF operates. Andre Spatz, UNICEF's CIO, explains:

> As a CIO, I invest a lot of my time in making governance work at all levels, to educate, coach, mentor and lobby. In a

global organization, governance is quite a challenge. We face high pressures for synergy across UNICEF and at the same time, we have high pressures for local autonomy from the regional and country offices. CIO leadership in a global IT organization is not just command and execute. We need to continually empower people with a vision and execution strategy, and position governance elements within a global framework. Part of my role is to ensure that we do not centralize too much and that our IT organization adapts to the different cultural environments we work in.[5]

Companies with effective IT governance have profits that are 20 percent higher than companies pursuing similar strategies.[6] But IT governance is a mystery to many key decision makers at most companies. Our research indicates that, on average, only 38 percent of senior managers in a company know how IT is governed. And ignorance is not bliss. Senior management's awareness of IT governance processes proved to be the best indicator of governance effectiveness. At top-performing firms, as many as 80 percent of senior executives are aware of how IT is governed.

In our study of almost three hundred companies around the world, we did not identify a single best formula for governing IT.[7] However, one thing is clear: effective IT governance doesn't happen by accident. Top-performing companies carefully design governance, and managers throughout those companies make daily decisions putting that design into practice.

Project Management

Project management has emerged as a critical competence in many, if not most, companies. Increasingly, companies are adopting standardized project methodologies—either homegrown or industry-developed approaches. A good project management methodology has well-defined process steps with clear deliverables to be reviewed at regular checkpoints, often called "gates." Many companies design metrics for assessing project performance and conduct postimplementation reviews to improve project managers' skills and the company's methodology.

IT-related projects have long been guided by a project life cycle. Variations of the life cycle define a set of four to eight project phases (e.g., proposal, requirements, specification, development, implementation, and change management), each with a specific set of objectives, deliverables, and metrics.[8] Good project management establishes a set of gates that check on projects' progress and assess their chances for meeting their goals. Companies may have as many as twelve to fifteen gates during a project. Disciplined project management processes are a necessary condition for good engagement. They ensure that all projects execute certain tasks at certain times.

Few companies have integrated project governance into their DNA like Raytheon.[9] Raytheon, the aerospace and defense company, has 80,000 employees worldwide with about 80 percent of revenue from government and defense. Raytheon also provides and manages nearly every air-traffic-control system around the world. About 30 percent to 40 percent of Raytheon's revenue is generated outside the United States. The company's customers are typically men and women in uniform (e.g., military, pilots). To manage the large number of programs within its seven semiautonomous business units, Raytheon has developed a single approach for all projects. Rebecca Rhoads, vice president and CIO, explains:

"When you have 8,000 programs, you very quickly develop a governance model that manages your exceptions. You have to have flawless execution. But if you start reviewing 8,000 programs every month to make sure you're okay and that you're executing properly, you'll never finish before you've got to start again. So we have a governance model and a structure that reviews the programs on an exception basis. We have scorecards and metrics and don't look at the program in detail unless it's triggered an exception on the scorecard."

Figure 6-2 presents a simplified version of Raytheon's integrated product development system (IPDS)—the multi-gate process for managing all projects at Raytheon. IPDS is used to develop any solution, whether it's big or small, or it's software, hardware, or integrated. Every project starts with a bidding process and ends at gate 10—the readiness review—after which Raytheon is ready to go into production. Gate 11 is the postimplementation review. The gates at the top of figure 6-2 are used to govern all projects at Raytheon. The boxes on the figure are the IT reviews that occur at each gate in IPDS. Below the boxes are the committees and processes monitoring the project from both business and IT perspectives.

For IT project governance Raytheon builds on what makes it a strong company—the ability to manage 8,000 programs. At each gate any project goes through a number of business and IT reviews. For example, project initiation triggers gate 5, start-up review, requiring approvals from the program management office and the enterprise architecture and standards council. The integration of IT project management into business project management meets companywide IT objectives of building a foundation for execution one project at a time.

Linking Mechanisms

Companies with effective IT governance and disciplined project management can still have ineffective IT engagement. The third essential ingredient of the IT engagement model is the linking mechanisms connecting companywide governance and projects. Good IT governance ensures that there's clear direction on how to evolve the company's foundation. Good project management ensures that projects are implemented effectively, efficiently, and in a

FIGURE 6-2

Project management at Raytheon

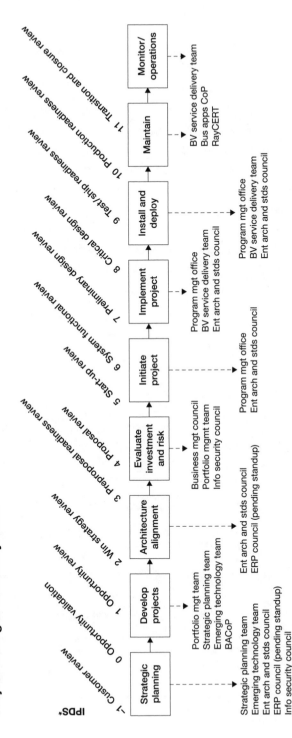

*IPDS = Integrated product development system

Note: BV (best value), Bus apps/BACoP (business applications community of practice), RayCERT (Raytheon computer emergency response team).

Source: Raytheon. Used with permission.

consistent manner to maximize learning. Good linking mechanisms ensure that projects incrementally build the company's foundation and that the design of the company's foundation (its operating model and enterprise architecture) is informed by projects.

Figure 6-3 describes three important types of linking mechanisms for any IT engagement model: architecture linkage, business linkage, and alignment linkage. These three types of linking mechanisms address the key alignment and coordination concerns of the company as long as key stakeholders take responsibility for them—and IT governance and project management are effective.

Architecture linkage establishes and updates standards, reviews projects for compliance, and approves exceptions. Architecture

FIGURE 6-3

Types of linking mechanisms

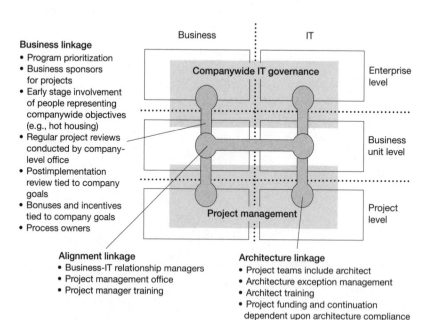

linkage connects the IT governance decisions about architecture with project design decisions. For example, a company working to increase integration may have a mechanism for insisting that a supply chain project—rather than focus narrowly on its own data needs—restructure an inventory database so that it facilitates anticipated future uses of the inventory data. Companies may fulfill architecture linkage with one mechanism, such as an architecture review board. More commonly, firms employ multiple mechanisms, ranging from architect training programs to architecture exception processes.

Similarly, *business linkage* ensures that business goals are translated effectively into project goals. Business linkage coordinates projects, connects them to larger transformation efforts, and focuses projects on attacking specific problems in the best possible way. For example, a key linking mechanism for companies pursuing companywide standardized processes is the use of process owners with primary responsibility for designing and updating processes. Business linkage also includes incentive programs to guide behavior as new projects demand new ways of thinking.

Alignment linkage mechanisms ensure ongoing communication and negotiation between IT and business concerns. Business-IT relationship managers or business unit CIOs are typically a critical linkage for translating back and forth between business goals and IT constraints. Other mechanisms in this category include a project management office, training and certification of project managers, and metrics for assessing projects.

Effective engagement models have all three types of linking mechanisms implemented via a few well-understood mechanisms. Earlier we noted that a company's management practices evolve through the stages of architecture maturity. Many of these evolving practices are linking mechanisms. As they are implemented and improved, they contribute to increasing sophistication of the IT engagement model. Over time, linking mechanisms can become increasingly embedded in IT governance and project management processes so that linking becomes an organizational habit.

A case study of Toyota Motor Marketing Europe illustrates how a company links its projects to higher-level objectives to build a foundation for execution one project at a time.

Toyota Motor Marketing Europe: Continuous Architecture Improvement

Toyota Motor Co. is one of the world's leading automobile manufacturers, offering a full range of models, from small passenger vehicles to trucks.[10] Toyota's global annual sales, combined with those of Hino and Daihatsu, totaled 7.5 million units in 2004, which generated almost $130 billion in net revenues. Toyota has forty-six manufacturing companies in twenty-six countries and regions, excluding Japan, and markets vehicles in more than 140 countries, supported by a consolidated workforce of 264,000 people.

Toyota Motor Europe is a holding company for Toyota Motor Marketing Europe (which handles the wholesale marketing of Toyota and Lexus vehicles, parts, and accessories in Europe) and Toyota Motor Engineering & Manufacturing Europe (which manages Toyota's European manufacturing and engineering operations).

Sales in Toyota's European operations increased 10 percent from 2003 to 2005 and represented 13.4 percent of total company revenues. Net income in Europe has revived from a loss in 2002 and small gain in 2003 to a respectable 6.3 percent of sales in fiscal year 2005.

Over the past ten years, Toyota Motor Marketing Europe's (TMME) operations have changed dramatically. European operations started as a central headquarters, handling only supply and demand management for Toyota's many independently managed country-based operations. As Toyota's sales grew in Europe, the management team realized it needed to take more control over operations if the company was to serve its European customers well. For example, before 1999 inventories of new cars were maintained within country-based units—a customer desiring a green Corolla with an automatic transmission would have to wait months to get it while that exact car could be just over the border, a few kilometers away. The same situation was true for repair parts. Management realized that TMME had to start acting like a single European entity rather than like individual country-based units.

Architecture Principles

To address this challenge, the IT unit in TMME has been working to build a foundation for execution to support a European operating model. Members of the architecture group did not find the company's European strategy statements specific enough to give them the direction they needed. So they surveyed the ongoing strategic initiatives to understand the operational capabilities that the company was trying to build. They condensed these into a simple statement that they used to guide the design of the architecture. Ludo Vandervelden, CIO and vice president of the vehicle logistics group, explained: "Complete customer satisfaction and the realization of cost reduction are the pillars around which we designed our customer-centric processes. Enterprise architecture is the road map to turn processes into efficient and effective solutions."[11]

From the statement of these desired capabilities, the architecture group designed a high-level set of architectural principles showing how each principle helped the company achieve its goals. These principles drove the architecture linking process for TMME. In 2000 the management team endorsed the principles. The IT unit then used the principles to start conversations with country-based units about the need to comply with a regional enterprise architecture. Peter Heinckiens, chief architect and deputy general manager of IT strategy, explained: "It was important to connect the architecture principles to the company's goals. If we were to talk to project managers only about architectural compliance, they would dismiss it. By connecting the architecture with the strategy of the company, we make architecture relevant. Now, if managers resist complying with the architecture, we simply point out that this means that they are not supporting Toyota's strategy. That changes the conversation."

Project Methodology

The architecture group then began implementation. After a few initial missteps, the group realized that the only way to effectively ensure that business projects didn't violate the architecture was to install a disciplined process for them and to assign an architect to each one (with some architects handling many different projects simultaneously). To introduce discipline into the project management process, the architecture group adapted and installed a standard project methodology.

Incentives

Heinckiens assigned a project architect to each team and created a unique reward system for these architects. The first and most basic requirement used to evaluate a project architect was whether his or her project succeeded. If the project was successful—even if it violated the architecture to some degree—the architect was judged to have "nearly achieved" his or her goals. If the project was successful, and the project helped implement the enterprise architecture, then the architect "fully achieved" goals. And if the project was successful, helped implement the enterprise architecture, and the architecture work resulted in improvements to the design of the overall enterprise architecture, then the architect "exceeded" goals. This focus on successful project delivery contributed to the project teams' acceptance of the project architects and further ensured that the architectural solutions were realistic and aligned with business goals. These changes facilitated the implementation of the architecture linkage at TMME.

Funding

Another key element of the engagement model at TMME was funding. The central architecture group had a limited pool of funds to support projects. For example, if a project had to connect to a spare-parts inventory database that required updating, then that project was given the task of updating the database and its interface. In some cases, this led to a higher project cost, which prompted the architecture group to look for other projects that also required interaction with that database to share the cost. If no other projects could be found, then the architecture group funded the extra development cost itself. Heinckiens explained: "If you have good engagement, most architecture efforts get funded through the projects. The projects need to do the work anyway, so all you're doing is asking them to do the work in an architecturally sound way. The cost of doing something right is usually no greater, and often leads to overall savings for the project."

Enforcement Authority

Another important component of TMME's engagement model is the authority to "pull the line" on a project. Because of the careful linkage of the architecture with the company's strategic goals and extensive education about the importance of architecture, the architecture team has gained the credibility and authority it needs to stop a project if necessary. This is an authority that is rarely used, but it is an integral part of the Toyota culture.[12] This option gives the architects some added power to achieve TMME's goals and adds weight to the architecture linking process.

Initial Appraisal

But the architecture group found that this level of engagement was not enough. Projects were commissioned that were fundamentally out of line with the enterprise architecture, and no amount of effort from the project architects could prevent architecture violations. The architecture group realized that it had to engage earlier in the project life cycle—it had to be involved in the creation of the project. Group members created a new first phase in the project methodology—called "appraisal"—in which the architecture group worked with the management team to ensure that the project was defined in a way that would support the enterprise architecture.

The appraisal phase now effectively achieves alignment linkage at TMME. For example, the IT group was asked to create a Web-based service to allow customers to select automotive accessories—steering wheel covers, gearshift knobs, and the like. The goal was to provide customers with pictures of the accessories and the ability to choose the ones they wanted. The architecture group realized that the underlying data was located in a number of places, including in an application whose vendor had gone out of business. Rather than build an application on top of this data structure, the architecture group worked with business managers to rescope the project and incorporate the design and construction of a new accessories database. The initial project only had to implement one small piece of this new database, but the design made it easy for future projects to finish the job. By being involved before the start of the project and rescoping the project, the architecture group helped push the architecture forward, without increasing the cost of the original project.

Outcomes

TMME measures the effectiveness of its architecture efforts with a number of metrics. It uses these metrics to measure the degree of architectural compliance of projects and how the architecture is contributing to business success. The technical architectural compliance of projects increased from 26 percent in 2001 to 93 percent in 2005. In addition, the company assessed the degree to which its enterprise architecture enabled strategic initiatives. The score on this assessment improved by 76 percent between 2001 and 2005.[13]

Toyota Motor Marketing Europe's engagement model has helped transform Toyota's European operations from a set of independent country-based units to a more integrated operating model. And the results have been positive: Toyota's European de-livery lead time for vehicles was reduced by 35 percent, and the inventory of spare parts was reduced by almost 50 percent. And Toyota's European unit sales have grown by more than 11 percent per year from 2001 through 2004.

What Is Good Engagement?

Independently and together, the three ingredients of engagement create business value. Without effective IT governance, there is no clarity about who makes what decision and how those people are held accountable. Without good project management, projects risk cost and schedule overruns and failure to meet objectives. Without effective linking mechanisms, there are no regular op-portunities to have discussions and make decisions about a proj-ect's ability to leverage the foundation and contribute to the foundation's evolution. Together, the engagement model ingredi-ents reinforce desirable behavior to create a foundation for execu-tion one project at a time.

Based on case study research at eighteen companies, we have identified some principles for ensuring that IT governance, proj-ect management, and linking mechanisms lead to successful engagement:

- *Clear, specific, and actionable objectives.* Effective IT engage-ment models clarify strategic objectives so standardization and integration requirements are clear. The first activity of TMME's architecture group was creating this clear state-ment and gaining top management's endorsement of it.

- *Motivation to meet company goals.* Formal incentives (e.g., bonus plans, annual reviews, and performance metrics) help focus business unit leaders and project managers on company, business unit, and project goals. For TMME, these were embodied in the reward systems of the project managers and project architects.

- *Enforcement authority.* Complementary to formal incentives are formal enforcements. Both help build an effort's credibility. Enforcement provides a process for changing, discontinuing, or granting an exception to a project that is not compliant with the target enterprise architecture. In several companies, the first project to actually get penalized for noncompliance (either by being delayed or losing funding) was an important tipping point that boosted the credibility of engagement efforts.

- *Early intervention and prevention.* Successful IT groups engage with business projects during the earliest stages of development to prevent bad solutions from being designed in the first place and to learn how to improve the target architecture. For example, Raytheon's IT organization engages with business projects in the first stages.

- *Transparent, regular, two-way communication.* With good engagement it is clear to everyone how the model works and who is involved. In addition, alignment and coordination are not simply achieved; they are maintained through regular dialogue between business and IT and across business units. This helps dispel perceptions that engagement processes are simply a way for the corporate center or IT to assert its will; it enables parties to learn from each other, negotiate differences, and develop a common understanding of the foundation for execution.

And, as noted in Chapter 5, the results of engagement can be profound. Companies whose architectural initiatives were strategically effective had architects on 81 percent of their project teams; less successful companies had architects on only 49 percent of teams. Successful companies reviewed significantly more of their projects for architectural compliance and involved more of their senior managers in the definition and oversight of architectural initiatives.

SOSCO: The Engagement Model in Action

One large U.S.-based software and services company had tradi-
tionally been structured to encourage business unit specialization.[14] The company, which we will call "SOSCO," had no agents
or branches. Instead, each business unit developed a call center with
specialized customer service representatives. When a new CEO
was hired in early 2000, he created a vision for a more integrated
operating model (a Coordination model, with high integration and
low standardization). IT management used this vision to develop
a new enterprise architecture. The new architecture specified that
SOSCO customers would gain access to the company's products
and services through multiple channels integrated through a standardized technology and data environment.

Designing IT Governance for Companywide Synergies

To implement the new vision for a more integrated firm, SOSCO
made structural changes emphasizing companywide processes. For
example, the business unit marketing departments were consolidated in a corporate marketing function. A key change was the
creation of a new companywide operations (CWO) unit. Headed by
an executive vice president, CWO is responsible for all companywide projects.

In addition to structural changes, SOSCO designed IT governance processes to encourage companywide synergies. SOSCO clarified IT decision rights for each of the key IT decisions (see table 6-2),
vesting decision-making responsibilities in five different groups:

1. *SOSCO's executive committee:* consists of the CEO, the presidents of the seven major operating companies, the CIO,
   and the head of CWO. This committee meets monthly to
   clarify companywide goals and distinguish company and
   business unit boundaries.

2. *Companywide operations:* defines and implements major projects reflecting the companywide goals specified by the executive committee. CWO has a staff of 275, including 15 program managers who coordinate multiple projects related to a single business process (e.g., customer relationship management).

3. *The IT unit:* headed by the corporate CIO. Business unit CIOs have dual reporting relationships—to the CIO and to the general managers of their business units. The IT unit designs shared IT services and delivers service-level agreements negotiated with each of the business units. The IT unit takes responsibility for ensuring that investments in the company's technical infrastructure move the company toward its foundation for execution.

4. *The architecture committee:* a subset of key technologists within the IT unit. The fifteen-member architecture committee defines technical standards and works with IT architects to identify common needs across the company's several hundred business unit and companywide projects.

5. *The investment steering committee:* establishes project priorities. Chaired by the executive vice president of CWO, this nine-member committee includes senior managers representing each of the major business units. In establishing project priorities, the committee considers the potential value to the company of both business-unit-specific and company projects. The committee also considers the availability of needed infrastructure and the readiness of the firm to effectively implement each project.

SOSCO ensures coordination of IT decisions through overlapping memberships in these decision structures. For example, CWO's executive vice president is on the executive committee and heads

TABLE 6-2

SOSCO's IT governance arrangements

IT decision	Process
IT principles	Executive committee of CEO, CIO, executive vice president of companywide operations (CWO), 7 business unit general managers
Enterprise architecture	Architecture committee of 15 senior technologists headed by CTO
IT infrastructure strategies	Senior IT management team
Business needs	CWO unit for companywide systems; business unit leaders for local systems
IT investment and prioritization	Investment steering committee of 9 senior managers, including IT, headed by executive vice president of CWO

© 2005 MIT Sloan Center for Information Systems Research. Used with permission.

the investment steering committee. Thus, as the executive committee defines company priorities, the executive vice president takes responsibility for reflecting those priorities in the funding decisions of the investment steering committee and the project designs of CWO.

Project Management

Each project at SOSCO follows a standard project development methodology mandating an eight-phase project life cycle. Every senior manager and project team member is familiar with the company's internally developed project methodology. Early phases of the project life cycle help determine the viability of the project—ability to implement, likelihood of receiving benefits, and availability of needed infrastructure. For companywide projects, management assigns a project sponsor in the key business unit as well as coleaders from CWO and the business unit.

Linkages Between IT Governance and Project Management

SOSCO has implemented a set of roles and processes at the project level to ensure that IT governance decisions are communicated to the projects and enacted throughout the firm. To link project management with IT governance, SOSCO has implemented the three major types of linking mechanisms to coordinate project goals with the company's overall goals and to achieve on-time, on-budget results.

The architecture linking mechanisms consist of a network of key decision makers, including project architects, CWO, and, with the most important projects, the CEO. Like TMME, SOSCO assigns an IT architect to each project team. These project architects are responsible for ensuring that individual projects are compliant with technology standards and that related projects reuse technologies as appropriate. If a project architect feels an exception to the standards is warranted, he or she either seeks approval from one of the assistant vice presidents authorized to grant exceptions or refers the request to the architecture committee.

CWO members lead companywide projects and take responsibility for the business linkage. In addition, to ensure that major projects are on track, the CEO meets with business unit presidents every month to review financials and discuss progress. These one-on-one meetings serve to identify the need for any senior management intervention, to reassess resource allocations and goals, and to avoid surprises in business unit or company outcomes. These meetings are an important business linkage mechanism.

Finally, the CEO encourages behavior consistent with his vision through a bonus program for all employees based on company goals. In 2004 every SOSCO employee—from the mailroom clerk to the top executive—received a 15 percent bonus to recognize achievement of those goals. Senior managers were also compensated for operating company results and their success in meeting their individual objectives. In this way, SOSCO has supported its engagement processes with an incentive system that rewards desired behavior.

IT governance and project management are explicitly connected via business, architecture, and alignment linking mechanisms. As a result, the project management process reinforces high-level governance decisions. Typically SOSCO spends only 2 percent of project expenses on projects eventually declared nonviable while delivering 99 percent of its projects on time and on budget.

Using Enterprise Architecture as an Organizational Compass

Describing the challenges of implementing an IT architecture, Jim Crookes, chief architect at BT, remarked: "Architecture implementation is like sailing. You have to use the energy of the wind, but it's not always blowing in the same direction you want to go. It's a lot easier to tack your way forward than to row into the teeth of the wind, which is what architects sometimes try to do. You have to use the momentum of business projects to get to where you want to go, even if it means you're not always heading directly toward your goal."[15]

Companies building a foundation for execution should use their enterprise architecture as a compass, directing the company toward its intended operating model. To stay on track these companies use an IT engagement model to influence the direction of projects and ensure that each project achieves both local and companywide objectives.

By embedding architectural improvements in projects, the costs of architectural transformation are spread over those projects with little incremental cost to individual ones. By engaging with projects early and regularly, a company can ensure that each project helps build out the architecture and that the architecture is realistic and aligned with company goals. Effective engagement ensures that all key stakeholders share the risks and responsibilities associated with changing business process and IT systems necessary for achieving companywide synergies. And with good engagement, the company ensures that the right foundation gets built steadily and reliably, one project at a time.

7

Use Enterprise Architecture to Guide Outsourcing

IN THE EARLY 1970S, Mazda and Isuzu entered the U.S. market for small pickup trucks. But rather than manufacturing the trucks themselves, they outsourced the final assembly to Ford and GM. Why? Because of the price of chickens in Germany.[1]

Ten years earlier, a trade war had erupted between the United States and West Germany over the sale of U.S. poultry in the West German market. Concerned about the health of its domestic industry, the European Economic Community, led by West Germany and France, designated poultry as an important growth industry and tripled the tariffs on U.S. poultry. Exports of U.S. chickens to Europe dropped from more than $30 million to less than $600,000. To retaliate, the United States slapped a tariff of 25 percent on "automobile trucks," targeting the import of VW cargo vans and pickup trucks. The sales of VW light trucks in the United States dropped by a third the following year and ended soon after.

When the Japanese entered the U.S. market ten years later, the "chicken tariff" found a new target. The Japanese realized that to avoid the tariff, they had to do the final assembly of their trucks in the United States. The cost of building assembly plants was prohibitive, so they found U.S. partners to help them. To this day, more than 99 percent of the light trucks on U.S. roads are assembled in the United States.

Like Japanese automakers, many companies find that for cost, regulatory, or other reasons, they have to outsource critical activities. IT and IT-enabled business processes are candidates for outsourcing, but the importance of a company's foundation for execution argues for exercising caution. Outsourcing can be a valuable approach to helping mature an architecture, but a company can lose ground if outsourcing is inappropriately applied. In this chapter we discuss how architecture can be a guide to outsourcing decisions.

Three Types of Outsourcing Relationships

Companies outsource IT and IT-enabled business processes for a number of reasons, including lower costs, variable capacity, risk mitigation, process reengineering, and the opportunity to focus on core capabilities. Consistent with other studies, our study of eighty outsourcing efforts found that executives most often cite variable capacity (almost 90% of respondents) and cost savings (more than 70%) as key objectives for outsourcing (figure 7-1).[2] Less than a third of executives cite objectives related more specifically to supporting architectural initiatives, such as process reengineering or business process discipline.

To understand the architectural implications of outsourcing, it's useful to recognize the differences between three types of outsourcing relationships: (1) a *strategic partnership,* in which an outsourcer takes on responsibilities for an integrated set of client operations; (2) a *cosourcing alliance,* in which the client and vendor share management responsibility for project success; and (3) a *transaction relationship,* in which an outsourcer executes a well-defined, repeatable IT or IT-enabled business process for a client. These three types of outsourcing relationships have different benefit-risk profiles (figure 7-2). Each also has different implications for enterprise architecture.

FIGURE 7-1

Outsourcing objectives

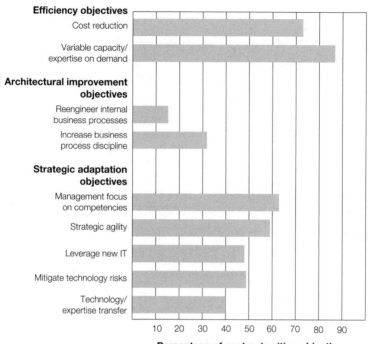

*Survey conducted of 80 outsourcing contracts. Results reflect number of contracts that cited objective as important (4) or very important (5) on a scale of 1 to 5.

© 2005 MIT Sloan Center for Information Systems Research and Cynthia M. Beath. Used with permission.

FIGURE 7-2

Three outsourcing models

	Three mutually exclusive outsourcing models		
	Strategic partnership	**Cosourcing**	**Transaction**
What is outsourced	Broad responsibility for operational activities	Project management and implementation	Narrowly defined, repeatable process
Key metrics	Bottom-line impact	Project success	Quality and/or cost per transaction
Client-vendor relationship	Negotiated accountability	Joint project management	Arm's length
Client expectations[a]	Cost savings; variable capacity; management focus on core competencies	Cost savings; access to expertise on demand	World-class processes; variable capacity; management focus on core competencies
Vendor offerings[b]	Capability to deliver broad range of specialized services; integration expertise; disciplined practices; economies of scale	Labor arbitrage; project management expertise; expertise on specialized technologies	Standard best practice process components; economies of scale; distinctive platforms or assets
Client success[c]	50%	63%	90%
Vendor success	50%	75%	90%

Decreasing risk ⟶

a. Client expectations based on 80 surveys of outsourcing success; there was a statistically significant relationship between the outsourcing model and the listed client expectations.
b. Derived from 8 case studies of company outsourcing experience.
c. Client views based on 80 surveys of outsourcing success. Statements presented: "Within the firm we view this outsourcing agreement as a success" and "The vendor is profiting from the outsourcing arrangement." Percentage is based on number of respondents who rated the statement as a 4 or 5 on a scale of 1 to 5.

© 2005 MIT Sloan Center for Information Systems Research and Cynthia M. Beath. Used with permission.

Strategic Partnerships

In a strategic partnership, vendors provide an integrated set of operational services. For example, a single strategic partnership deal might encompass mainframe operations, WAN and LAN management, telephony, Web hosting, and help desk services. Similarly, outsourcing of an IT-intensive function like human resource management can include processes such as reward and recognition, learning and development, employee documentation, and advisory services.[3] By integrating service offerings, the vendor adds value beyond the value of the individual services.

How strategic partnerships build a foundation for execution

Strategic partnerships should allow companies to focus on core capabilities while a vendor handles major operational responsibilities.[4] Strategic partnerships often deliver cost savings (at least initially) by introducing more disciplined processes and by providing variable capacity to limit a company's need to build excess capacity. Vendors profit from strategic partnerships by leveraging economies of scale and scope, unique expertise, and disciplined management practices. Despite the potential for mutual benefit, these deals are risky. In our study only 50 percent of strategic partnerships were viewed as successful by the client company.

Metrics are part of the problem. While vendors expect to earn a margin on the integrated set of services, clients often assess their partners based on the price and performance of each individual service-level agreement. If the client's management practices are sloppy, the vendor can introduce efficiencies, and both parties can realize value from the relationship. However, some of the efficiencies are realized only if clients forgo entrenched behaviors. In IT partnerships many companies struggle with behavior changes that require adhering to technology standards or limiting the number of discretionary changes to systems and system schedules. Without behavioral changes, there may not be enough real savings for both client and vendor to achieve their bottom-line objectives.

The behavior changes necessary for outsourcing success are also required for building a foundation for execution. Strategic partnerships involving IT or IT-intensive functions (e.g., human resources, accounting) engage external experts in the process of defining and implementing standardized technologies and management practices. For companies in the Business Silos stage or early in the Standardized Technology stage, vendors' best practices will inevitably lead to consolidation of existing technical platforms and a reduction in the variety of technologies in use. A strategic partnership forces a shared-services mentality, requiring business leaders to come to agreement on which services will be provided centrally and which will be provided locally. Of course, companies can introduce shared services without external assistance, but they need expertise and a commitment to continuously improving their administrative functions.

A strategic partnership is particularly valuable early in stage 2 (Standardized Technology) because it helps move a company toward increased standardization. In an effective partnership, the client benefits from world-class operations without having to invest in the development of world-class skills. Campbell Soup Co. provides an example of how such partnerships can work to help a company develop its foundation for execution.

Case study of a strategic partnership: Campbell Soup Co.

Campbell Soup Co., a $7 billion food company, sells more than just soup.[5] Its brands in the United States include Pepperidge Farm, Godiva, V8, Pace, and Prego as well as Campbell's. In FY 2004, Campbell had approximately 24,000 employees in twenty-two countries and earned $647 million (an increase of 8.7% over FY 2003).

At the turn of the last century, Campbell, like other companies in the consumer packaged-food industry, was experiencing competitive pressures from many sides. Consumers were both price and health conscious. Significant consolidation in the industry meant that Campbell, a medium-sized firm, competed in an industry dominated by giants such as Kraft, Unilever, and Nestlé. Moreover, Campbell's upstream agribusiness partners and downstream retail partners were consolidating and, as a result, had become increasingly powerful in their dealings with Campbell and its peers. Meanwhile, the downstream retailers were increasing their offerings in private-label foods.

In 2002 CEO Doug Conant committed to moving Campbell from a Diversification operating model (low standardization and low integration) to a Unification model (high standardization and high integration). His planned transformation had huge implications for IT, and he brought in Doreen Wright as senior vice president and the company's first corporate CIO, to address the IT challenge. According to Wright:

> Looking at the IT function is like having the company look at itself in the mirror: Whatever's wrong with the company will show up in the IT function. Clearly, Campbell had been run as a portfolio of independent businesses—too independent. Similarly, the various IT groups were independent . . . We were a hodgepodge of disparate computing platforms and network protocols without an enterprise [architecture]. We had every conceivable technology running somewhere. [We were] a confederation of global IT groups, with little or no governance and an inflexible IT infrastructure that was very costly to support.

To transform itself, Campbell's management team pursued a strategy of distinguishing between core and noncore business activities. The company is managing core activities—sales, marketing, R&D, retail execution, trade management, and product life cycle management—for differentiation and growth. In contrast, Campbell is managing noncore activities for low cost. Outsourcing is one approach to managing those noncore activities. Wright says:

Because we are trying to transform ourselves, not just from a technology perspective, but much more importantly from a business perspective, the thing that I need more than anything else is management capacity. I need the capacity of my staff to introduce the new, to understand it, and keep up. I've got business people clamoring to do data synchronization and collaborative planning with our customers, and introducing new R&D capabilities, and trade promotion capabilities, all of that kind of stuff. The last thing I want to soak up my leaders' heads with is the running of the computers themselves. I need everybody's mind on introducing the new. So, I completely outsource the infrastructure. The running of infrastructure is all done by IBM. The maintaining of the legacy applications is probably seventy-five percent outsourced. In almost all cases, I hire a third party as my integrator. That doesn't mean we don't have a high level of involvement, but I have the expertise of a partner who knows how to integrate.

Consistent with its business strategy, the IT unit at Campbell has adopted an "IS Lite" organization model.[6] In an IS Lite model many traditional IT services (applications development, maintenance, and computer operations) are outsourced. Technical governance, strategy (i.e., architecture), and shared infrastructure are centralized for coherence and cost-efficiency. Relationship management, business process analysis, and solution delivery are localized in the businesses to ensure business alignment and speed to market.

Between 2002 and 2004 Campbell moved its architecture from stage one (Business Silos) to late stage 2 (Standardized Technology). With the help of IBM, its strategic partner, Campbell achieved virtually 100 percent global commonality with respect to standards, networks, and e-mail. Except for some international facilities, the company is running common operating systems, platforms, and middleware. This standardization has reduced IT unit costs; improved IT service quality, reliability, and security; improved IT's alignment and relationships with the business; and strengthened vendor relationships. From 2002 to 2004, IT banked nearly $5 million in one-time savings and $8 million in annual savings. CIO Wright credits more than half of the annual savings to various adjustments in Campbell's sourcing arrangements, including improved service levels at no additional cost and various cost-saving upgrades, migrations, and replacements.

Despite the cost savings, Wright believes the real value of outsourcing lies elsewhere: "There are things that you do as a company which are critical. You couldn't run your company without them, but they should not differentiate you. They should be as standard as possible. And if you can find someone who can do it as well or better at an equal or lower cost, why would you not do that? What you would get out of that is management capacity to focus on the things that are core and differentiating to your company."

Campbell is now moving its architecture into stage 3 (Optimized Core). To achieve this transition, the company has engaged IBM to lead its implementation of an ERP system. With a reliable, secure infrastructure as a base, Campbell managers will take responsibility for business process design and for changing organizational behaviors. IBM project managers will lead the technical side of the implementation. To make this arrangement work, both parties have made a long-term commitment to enhance Campbell's IT capabilities. Says Wright:

> You know, if I were providing my own data center services, I would blow it sometimes. I would make bad decisions. It is not different when you have an outsourcer. What is important is that the two sides are each deriving benefits, that they trust each other, and that each gives and takes. A good number of our IBM people, including the manager, sit right with us in Camden [New Jersey]. The manager reports to the Campbell CTO and is at every

staff meeting. They have obviously signed confidentiality agreements. They have access to our business and IT strategic plans, and the senior IBM partner has strong relationships with many of our business leaders, in addition to me. They have a huge vested interest in this company. They want us to win like we want us to win, and there is a very, very high level of trust.

An effective strategic partnership involves constant negotiation around inevitable changes in business and technology. Clients need vendors to adapt their offerings and processes to changing business conditions; vendors need clients to adjust their behaviors to permit appropriate process innovations and service changes. Successful partnerships like the Campbell-IBM partnership often apply a first-choice provider principle, meaning that the strategic partner is favored (although not always chosen) when new activities are to be outsourced. This reduces search costs for the client and sales costs for the vendor—and it encourages both partners to focus on strategic value, not just lower costs, from the outsourcing arrangement.

As the Campbell case shows, a strategic partnership can continue to reap benefits beyond stage 2, as managers in the client company focus on addressing new strategic opportunities, rather than ongoing operations. But a stage 3 relationship may benefit even more from a cosourcing alliance.

Cosourcing Alliances

In a strategic alliance, responsibilities are assigned clearly to one partner. The client and vendor define boundaries distinguishing the responsibilities of each party. In a cosourcing alliance, clients and vendors share responsibilities, usually in a project-oriented environment. Team members from both client and vendor converge and form a team to meet a business objective. Cosourcing is a growing model for delivering new systems and processes that demand both business and technology expertise.

For example, one large financial services company has engaged an offshore company to handle much of its development. The vendor partner has brought project management staff to the client's site so that teams comprise client staff, and on-site and offshore vendor staff. As is typical of cosourcing alliances, this relationship draws on both the client's deep business knowledge and the vendor's specialized skills in technology and project management.[7]

How cosourcing alliances build a foundation for execution

Client interest in cosourcing arises from the desire to access technical and project management expertise on an as-needed basis. In addition, clients see opportunities for cost savings in their alliances. Vendors meet these demands by building project management, industry, and technical expertise and then leveraging that expertise across multiple projects with multiple clients. Vendors meet client demands for cost savings by adding offshore resources to their talent pools. A cosourcing alliance allows a client firm to rely on a core set of project team members—some internal, some external. In response to shifts in project loads, clients rely on vendors to provide supplemental resources. Vendors build in protections against extreme and unanticipated variations but can normally shift talent between clients.

Cosourcing alliances are not as risky as strategic partnerships. In our study 63 percent of clients felt their alliance was successful, and 75 percent felt the vendor was making money on the relationship (figure 7-2). The risks of cosourcing can be managed through negotiation of accountabilities. As with strategic partnerships, however, metrics can be a challenge. In an effective alliance, both the vendor and client populate project teams. While the project leader—often from the vendor—is ultimately accountable for the outcome, it is a team that delivers (or doesn't deliver). Thus, the contribution of the outsourcer in a cosourcing alliance is diffi-cult to isolate from the contribution of the client's employees. Dow Chemical, which deploys project teams with, on average, four ven-dor employees for every internal team member, has a set of met-rics to assess team productivity on factors such as function points. But ultimately, the CIO notes, the measure of success for the out-sourcing arrangement is the project outcome. He considers his al-liance a success because alliance teams consistently deliver high functionality on time and on budget.

Cosourcing proves particularly valuable for companies in the third architecture maturity stage (Optimized Core). Companies at-tempting to integrate their data and standardize their processes often have to rip out legacy systems and replace those systems with new ones with which they have little experience (e.g., ERP systems, Web services, customer relationship management sys-tems, enterprise application integration software). Rather than in-ternally develop expertise in these new technologies, companies can rely on experienced third parties.[8] Vendors can help imple-ment, maintain, upgrade, and where necessary, link to other tech-nologies. They can also help with process-reengineering efforts. With this kind of help from a vendor, the client can focus man-agement attention on the organizational changes necessary to im-plement more standardized and integrated environments.

Cosourcing alliances can take a variety of forms. Liverpool Di-rect Ltd. (LDL) is a cosourcing alliance established as a joint ven-ture between Liverpool City Council and BT. The case provides an example of how a cosourcing alliance allowed an organization (in this case a local government) to achieve improved processes, lower costs, and architecture maturity.

Case study of a cosourcing alliance: Liverpool Direct Ltd.

Liverpool, the sixth-largest city in the United Kingdom, is fa-mous as the home of the Beatles and Liverpool Football Club.[9] Once a dominant trading center, Liverpool fell on hard times during the second half of the twentieth century. The shipping industry, in which it had its roots, was in decline. The city's population of 468,000 was decreasing. The outward migration of younger, skilled people had resulted in a higher proportion of dependent people. In 1998, 33 percent of the population was unemployed, retired, or unable to work.

David Henshaw, who became chief executive of Liverpool City Council (LCC) in October 1999, inherited an organization in collapse. Out of 426 local authorities, LCC was third from the bottom in terms of service quality, and it had the highest local tax in the United Kingdom. Delivery of social services such as housing, medical care, educational support, and financial benefits was slow, error-prone, and inefficient.

Henshaw was charged with achieving the city council's goal of "making Liverpool a premier European city again." He wanted to reengineer the council's services around the needs of its customers, stripping out bureaucracy and focusing on frontline service delivery. IT was integral to this vision of improving service, quality, and cost.

In 2001, to deliver new processes and underlying technology support, LCC entered the joint venture with BT. LDL took responsibility for five services, cosourced with LCC: (1) revenues and benefits, (2) HR, (3) payroll, (4) information technology, and (5) call center functions. LDL was managed via a joint venture board made up of the CEO, four BT directors, and two LCC representatives. Staff (30 from BT and 880 from LCC) who joined LDL reported to LDL management but, partly to appease union requirements, remained employees of their respective companies, with their existing salary and benefits.

According to the joint venture and shareholders agreement, LCC paid the joint venture £30 million a year for the ten years of the contract. This annual payment represented LCC's estimate of how much it would cost the council to run the five services cosourced with LDL. The annual £30 million payment covered the salaries of LCC employees and the interest on an operating lease, a financial arrangement that allowed BT to spread its agreed-upon investment in IT over the life of the contract. BT is entitled to the remainder of the annual payment to cover its own costs and generate a profit.

LDL's first move was to rationalize and standardize the IT infrastructure. Standards for hardware were defined for all new PCs and peripherals. Staff began to consolidate the council's 500 different databases into a single database. Software standards ensured compatibility between services and facilitated the transfer of information.

More important, LDL improved the delivery of city services to residents. In the revenues and benefits department, LDL reengineered business processes and introduced a document management system. These changes reduced the department's backlog from 60,000 queries to 4,000—a reduction of about a year's worth of work. Revenue collection also improved, resulting in an estimated gain of £1.5 million from high-rent debtors who had disputes with the council. LDL implemented a new customer relationship management system to redirect most resident inquiries to the call center. By June 2002 the call center handled and resolved 90 percent of inquiries at the first point of contact. Abandoned calls dropped from 25 percent to 12 percent. In parallel, the service grew from 80 seats taking 40,000 calls per month during office hours to a 24/7 operation, with 225 seats handling 160,000 calls. LDL also implemented an ERP system to replace the old paper-based processes in HR and payroll. The new system offered self-administration of transactions via an intranet and reduced the number of staff by 50 percent.

The benefits of this partnership were obvious for the council. The number of council staff was reduced from 23,500 to 19,800 while the quality of services sharply improved; 75 percent of the council's key performance indicators improved from rock bottom to the upper quartile of local government performance. Moreover, LCC was able to announce a 3 percent reduction in council tax. Increased morale resulted in a six-day cut in annual absenteeism rates, from sixteen days to the national average of ten days per person. The council expected these benefits to grow over time.

Although most cosourcing alliances don't have a formal joint venture arrangement, all cosourcing alliances depend on the efforts of joint client-vendor teams. Cosourcing can help companies standardize technologies in the second stage of architecture maturity (as in the case of Liverpool City Council), but cosourcing alliances are particularly valuable for helping companies through stage 3 (Optimized Core). It is in stage 3 that a vendor can provide IT expertise, business process design, and project management support to assist with the transformation to more standardized and integrated business processes. Yet as companies move into the fourth stage (Business Modularity) and rely more on external processes for their plug-and-play environments, cosourcing may give way to more transaction relationships.

Transaction Relationships

Transaction relationships—sometimes called "out-tasking"—outsource specific services like accounts payable processing, expense reporting, desktop provisioning, backup, and disaster recovery. Like strategic partnerships, transaction relationships assign clear responsibility to the vendor for executing the outsourced processes, but they are much more narrowly defined, arm's-length relationships. Transaction relationships outsource not only business process and IT support but also ownership of the software and the design of the process. Transaction relationships are appropriate for activities guided by clear business rules that are common across many organizations.

Benefits and risks of transaction relationships

Transaction relationships enjoy statistically significantly greater satisfaction than either of the other types of relationships. Respondents in our study considered their transaction outsourcing to be a success for both client and vendor in 90 percent of cases. Clients have three key objectives in their transaction relationships: access to best practices, variable capacity, and the ability to redirect management attention to core capabilities. Vendors address those needs by developing best practices, implementing and supporting standardized platforms, and developing economies of scale.

Where feasible, vendors also build unique assets or expertise. These capabilities allow them to improve service and lower costs. For example, eFunds Corp., which provides a range of outsourcing services to financial institutions, telecommunications companies, and retail organizations, has built a large database of credit information that is the key to its credit-checking process. This distinctive asset—which clients either cannot or would not replicate—helps protect the vendor's margins while providing a valued service to clients.

Successful transaction relationships have low management overhead. Customization, protracted contract negotiations, or client interference with how the vendor performs the process increases cost and undermines benefits for both parties. Conversely, a hands-off transaction relationship can deliver hassle-free, high-quality services to clients and reasonable margins to vendors.

As long as a process can be isolated from other company activities, companies can implement transaction outsourcing relationships at any architectural stage. For example, processes like personal computer configuration, business travel arrangements, and employee benefits processing are good candidates for outsourcing in early architecture maturity stages.

Transaction outsourcing cannot become strategically important or widely adopted until the Business Modularity stage. It is in this stage that companies have developed sufficient business process expertise to be able to extract and outsource those activities to which they can and should apply industry standards while retaining those activities that are necessarily unique. In addition, premature adoption of transaction outsourcing involves creating new interfaces to connect to each new vendor, whereas companies with mature architectures will adopt increasingly standardized, low-maintenance interfaces to their data and systems. A more mature architecture will also enable secure access to data; otherwise, risks will multiply as the number of interfaces grows.

Transaction outsourcing, as applied in stage 4, allows a company to plug external processes into a solid foundation for execution. Dow Chemical offers an example of a company designing its foundation for execution to readily implement transaction outsourcing relationships.

Case study of transaction relationships: Dow Chemical

In chapter 2 we discussed Dow Chemical's highly integrated and standardized operating model.[10] This operating model gives Dow very cost-effective and reliable global business processes. Dow has built this foundation for execution with extensive help from vendors. A cosourcing alliance with Accenture has, since 1996, supplemented Dow's own capabilities in application development and support. Since 2000, Dow has relied on a strategic partnership to manage computer operations. Management credits IBM with providing cost benefits through its economies of scale and with giving Dow the benefits of world-class infrastructure management without forcing in-house development of a capability that would prove to be neither rare nor distinctive.

Dow's foundation for execution has been less valuable, however, in supporting growth. Dow management expects that much of the company's future growth will come through joint ventures (JVs). President and CEO Andrew Liveris cites the benefits of joint ventures as "lower capital intensity, access to regional expertise and advantaged feedstocks; the ability to leverage our technology and know-how; and accelerated penetration in high-growth markets."[11] In 2004 Dow's approximately one hundred JVs accounted for 25 percent of the company's earnings. But JVs cannot rely on a highly integrated, highly standardized IT and business process environment. Dow needs modules that can be assembled as-needed while protecting the boundaries between itself and the JV. Frank

Luijckx, senior director of information systems strategy and architecture, explains:

> Today's IT architecture [at Dow], which is a monolithic architecture, is sometimes referred to as the castle. Within the castle, things are really nice. It's very secure, people work together very well, there is plenty of food, and we are generating a lot of value. But if there is somebody that we want to work with, we always have to bring them in the castle, right? Because the perimeter defense is on the outside of the castle. I don't mean just the security—it's reporting, everything. And within the castle, we don't have any rooms with doors. So, if we bring in a joint venture that we want to work closely with, we have to bring them in the castle and trust them. And you can't do that. It is only a question of time before you are going to bring somebody in and it is not going to work, or where somebody else will say, yes, I know you trust them, but we don't, we don't think this is a good relationship.[12]

To support its JVs and to move into a more modular environment, Dow is gradually implementing a concept it calls the "Federated Broker Model" (FBM). In this model Dow purchases services from vendors who provide commodity business processes from their own systems. For example, Dow is planning to purchase ERP services rather than maintain ERP systems. These services will offer integration across companies instead of solely within companies, allowing Dow to selectively integrate processes with its JVs and other partners and customers. As Michael J. Costa, corporate director of six sigma and work process expertise at Dow, explains: "The vision of the Federated Broker Model is that we shift workflow into the BSP [business service provider], ASP [application service provisioning], BPO [business process outsourcing] area that is emerging. You enjoy a much more competitive pricing environment because now it is not the SAPs and the PeopleSofts and the Oracles that control how companies work. It is more of a battle among providers on open platforms."

In the ideal state of the FBM vision, Dow will maintain its valuable horizontal and vertical integration, but it will no longer buy, build, or run applications. Nor will Dow buy individual components from individual providers—a scenario entailing significant management overhead. Instead, Dow managers envision buying application functionality from a strategic alliance that will bundle hardware, network, desktop, software, and process capability (combinations of ASP and BPO providers) into an integrated service model, giving Dow—and any other company—a single point of contact for this bundle. This alliance, not Dow, will choose the technology and make IT investments. Dow will pay for process-enabling functionality as needed.

Dow management recognizes that vendors are not yet able to meet the FBM's requirements. According to Dave Kepler, Dow's corporate vice president for shared services and CIO:

> One of the realities is to recognize the marketplace and what you can leverage and where there are things that you're going to have to really design yourself and use. We have to be very practical about the fact that the service providers will have a fair amount of volatility. So, the Federated Broker Model isn't an end state as much as it is a recognition that, boy, we can't develop all the software and we will try to leverage these variable services that we need. That means we're going to have to have a lot of interfaces and be pretty flexible in what we're trying to do.

While waiting for this market to emerge, Dow has implemented a few capabilities reflecting the promise of the Federated Broker Model, including outsourcing expense reporting to Bank of America, outsourcing 401(k) and stock options to Fidelity and Smith Barney, and outsourcing functions like payroll and elements of transportation logistics. Dow managers believe the Federated

Broker Model will win converts as fast as vendors can produce useful and affordable process modules. Dow is transforming from stage 3 (Optimized Core) to stage 4 (Business Modularity), and outsourcing is a big part of that transformation.

Few companies are ready to embark on transaction-processing relationships on the scale that Dow Chemical is currently pursuing. Dow's expertise in managing global process integration and standardization—its development of a stage 3 foundation for execution—has positioned the company to seize business process services as they become available in the marketplace. Other companies will outsource the small set of processes that are easily extracted from the business core (e.g., employee benefits, travel services) while they mature their architectures and build their foundations for execution.

Aligning Outsourcing Relationships with Architecture Stages

Dow Chemical demonstrates that a company can become competent in all three types of outsourcing relationships. But it is important to match the objectives and the services outsourced with the appropriate type of relationship. Clients and vendors in strategic partnerships who refuse to adapt to the strategic needs of their partners will become embroiled in bitter contract battles. Companies managing transaction relationships like strategic partnerships incur expensive and unnecessary overhead. And cosourcing that is treated like anything but a team environment is sure to suboptimize outcomes.

A company's ability to capitalize on the potential benefits of outsourcing to build a foundation for execution is, at least in part, dependent on an awareness of how outsourcing will contribute to, or leverage, enterprise architecture. Each of the three types of outsourcing relationships can help companies build their foundation for execution. But each contributes to architecture maturity in a different way. Figure 7-3 identifies how outsourcing contributes to architecture maturity.

FIGURE 7-3

Different outsourcing relationships are suited to different stages

	Business Silo	Standardized Technology	Optimized Core	Business Modularity
What to outsource	Easily isolated processes ────────────────────────────►	IT infrastructure management ────────────────────►	Project management of major systems implementations ──────►	Process design and operation with supporting technology
Ideal relationship	Narrowly focused transaction outsourcing ──────────────────────────►	Strategic partnership ────────────────────────────►	Cosourcing alliance ──────────►	Transaction outsourcing
Achievable outsourcing objectives	Cost savings	IT management discipline; cost savings; risk reduction; management focus	Technology/ expertise transfer; process discipline and reengineering; management focus; cost-effectiveness; variable capacity; risk sharing	Strategic agility; leverage IT and process expertise for world-class business processes; variable capacity; management focus; cost-effectiveness; risk sharing

© 2005 MIT Sloan Center for Information Systems Research and Cynthia M. Beath. Used with permission.

Outsourcing for Architecture Maturity

While outsourcing can facilitate maturation of an enterprise architecture, it cannot radically transform the company as the architecture matures. The technical challenges of architecture can be transferred, at least in part, to a vendor. But those technical challenges will be replaced with relationship management challenges. And the organizational change challenges are in no way diminished. The bottom line is: you can outsource to support the building of your foundation for execution, but you shouldn't outsource your architecture. The management practices listed in chapter 5 remain the responsibility of every company looking to evolve its architecture.

We noted at the start of the chapter that modular, plug-and-play companies are likely to become the norm. However, this model is only beginning to emerge and, thus, will not become the norm in most industries for quite some time. This is good news because it means that companies have time to learn how to change, how to move incrementally through the architecture stages, and how to implement outsourcing as appropriate vendor services become available.

8

Now—Exploit Your Foundation for Profitable Growth

IN THE AUTO INDUSTRY, companies could once succeed by developing a single popular car model. A popular car like the Volkswagen Beetle, the Dodge Caravan, or the Saab 900 would keep the profits rolling in for years. But the terms of competition have changed. No longer is it enough to do a single car well; to succeed a car company has to develop a great *platform* of models. Companies now have to develop a family of products that share the same chassis, engine, and drivetrain but appeal to different market segments. Thus when Volkswagen introduced the new Beetle, it used the same platform as the VW Golf, Audi TT Coupe, and other models.[1]

Like a car platform, a foundation for execution must serve more than one business need. Executives must look to leverage their foundation in new and innovative ways. In a business environment in which China is the world's factory and India is the world's service provider, and where the market sells world-class business processes for anyone to use, companies must continually evolve and exploit a foundation for execution to support new business activities. Companies that fail to build, or continuously augment, a foundation for execution will not be able to grow—or more accurately, they will not be able to grow profitably.

There are two general strategies for profitable growth: organic growth and acquisition-driven growth. A good foundation for execution helps with both. For organic growth, a solid foundation helps companies leverage—rather than re-create—technology platforms and business process expertise. Instead of inventing capabilities for each new business opportunity, a company can apply existing capabilities, allowing faster response and greater profitability.

Companies pursuing growth through mergers and acquisitions can also leverage their foundations. In this case, companies have a choice of two strategies: to "rip and replace" or to diversify. Rip-and-replace companies use their foundation to drive a transformation of the acquired company, leveraging their best practices in the combined entity. Companies using a diversification strategy allow their acquisitions to use their existing foundations. They gain synergy through standardized technology and shared services.

This chapter uses case studies to show how companies can grow profitably by building and leveraging a foundation for execution. We end the chapter with our forecast for the next stage of architecture maturity and the benefits it will offer companies.

Leveraging the Foundation for Profitable Growth

Companies become more agile as they move their foundations through the different stages of architecture maturity. A company's operating model dictates the route it takes to architecture maturity and the benefits it achieves. Three companies with three different operating models—UPS, MetLife, and 7-Eleven Japan—show the different types of agility companies develop to achieve profitable growth.

Profitable Growth in a Unification Model

In a Unification operating model, companies leverage standard-ized IT infrastructure, standardized business processes, and shared data. As a company matures its enterprise architecture, the foun-dation gets thicker—more of its repetitive processes are digitized end-to-end. This strong base facilitates profitable growth when line managers use the integrated data to better serve customers and se-nior managers turn their attention to new markets, products, or process innovations.

As described earlier, UPS has been leveraging its foundation to create agility around its core package delivery business.[2] This agility allows the company to regularly create new products and services. During the 1990s, UPS grew its revenues from $14 billion to $30 billion. Revenues in 2004 exceeded $36 billion. UPS deliv-ered 3.6 billion packages in 2004, an increase of 4 percent over the prior year. In the past five years, UPS has consistently outperformed the Dow Jones Industrial Average, the Standard & Poor's 500, and its major competitors. One reason is that UPS's operating margin was nearly three times the industry average and 50 percent higher than Federal Express's. In 2004 UPS was named by *Fortune* maga-zine as the most admired company in its industry for the sixth consecutive year.

UPS's growth has stemmed from its agility to leverage economies of scale and to innovate to extend its core. For example, UPS started using the Internet for package tracking and customer communica-tions as early as 1995. Next, UPS gave customers tracking software that many linked to their homegrown purchasing and distribution systems. But as customers bought ERP systems to handle their pur-chasing and distribution needs, they could no longer use UPS's tracking software. So, the company established alliances with key vendors, like Oracle, Peoplesoft, Harbinger, IBM, and SAP, who built the UPS tracking interface into their enterprise systems soft-ware, making it easier for customers to do business—much more business—with UPS.

Similarly, UPS has gradually implemented processes to leverage its investment in its delivery information acquisition device (DIAD). Introduced in 1991—and upgraded in 1993, 1999, and 2005—this device captures a customer signature with every delivery and then uploads the data in real time to the package information database. The device was initially justified on the basis of cost savings: each driver saved about thirty minutes per day, time formerly spent summarizing the day's activities. With 60,000 drivers, the cost savings represented by one half hour per person were significant, but the real value of the DIAD was in the additional information collected about each package and customer. This information contributed to better understanding of the profitability of individual customers and packages. The company used this information to make routing and pricing decisions and, ultimately, to provide UPS customers with new services based on their individual shipping habits.

UPS has continued to add more capabilities to its foundation for execution, increasing the company's efficiency and agility. UPS's systems now dictate where packages are placed on the truck, the order in which packages are delivered, and how drivers record a delivery. Because its delivery processes are digitized, drivers have little discretion in these tasks. But the precision of the company's delivery practices leads to greater efficiency and predictability, and minimizes the time managers spend on operational issues, allowing them to turn their attention to product and service innovations, as described in chapter 1.

Digitization limits UPS's ability to change its core delivery process, but the company can easily take on new customers—and the employees who serve those customers—knowing that its own new employees will perform to the same high standard because they are trained to use the same systems. UPS has further leveraged its IT infrastructure and business process foundation by expanding globally. UPS's international business, which constituted 15 percent of revenues in 1999, has grown at double-digit rates ever since.

Profitable Growth in a Replication Model

In a Replication operating model, companies leverage standardized IT-enabled business processes to grow into new markets and increase products and services. As a company matures its enterprise architecture, it expands the number of processes and systems in its foundation. These digitized processes readily support new products and services. When Replication companies move their foundation for execution into a new market, automation reduces start-up costs, so the revenue base can expand profitably. Seven-Eleven Japan is a Replication company that has leveraged its foundation to grow profitably.

Seven-Eleven Japan (SEJ) has built its Replication foundation for execution around its product-mix capabilities.[3] Using this foundation, SEJ grew from 6,000 to 10,000 stores between 1997 and 2005 while maintaining its position as the most profitable retailer in Japan.

CEO Toshifumi Suzuki describes his vision of SEJ's stores as follows: "[They're] stores where you can find a solution for any of your daily life problems. We always try to plan and design a store in such a way that our store neighbors, in particular, can get whatever they need at any time they want."[4]

Suzuki believes that one of the most serious problems in retail is a missed opportunity to sell an item because it is out of stock. Accordingly, ever since he opened his first store in 1974, Suzuki has focused on maintaining optimum product mix. Since the late seventies, SEJ has built and exploited IT-enabled processes supporting item-level control—meaning that the items on the shelf in any given store have been precisely selected for customers of that store. With the goal of better customer service, SEJ has, over the past thirty years, evolved its IT, inventory management, and distribution capabilities. The lower half of figure 8-1 describes the evolution of the technologies and distribution processes that cumulatively built SEJ's foundation for execution.

FIGURE 8-1

7-Eleven Japan creates more value each year

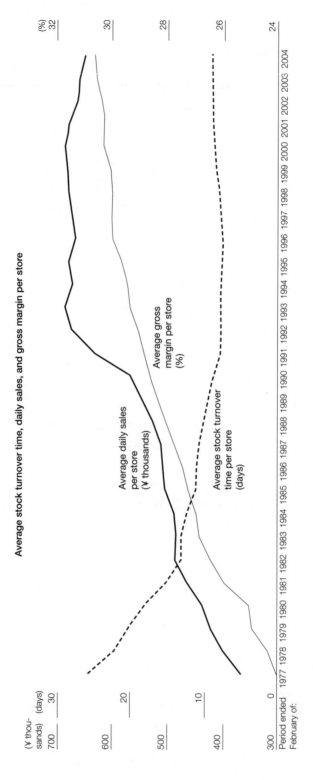

Average stock turnover time, daily sales, and gross margin per store

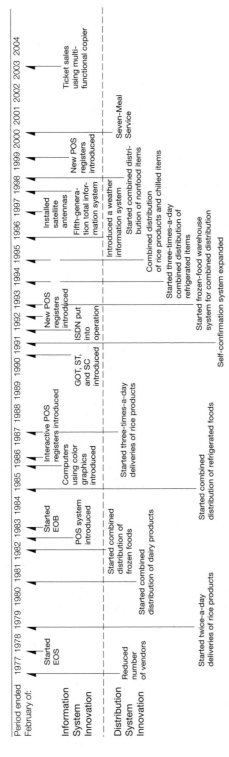

Period ended February of:	1977	1978	1979	1980	1981	1982	1983	1984	1985	1986	1987	1988	1989	1990	1991	1992	1993	1994	1995	1996	1997	1998	1999	2000	2001	2002	2003	2004

Information System Innovation

- Started EOS
- POS system introduced
- Started EOB
- Computers using color graphics introduced
- Interactive POS registers introduced
- GOT, ST, and SC introduced
- ISDN put into operation
- New POS registers introduced
- Fifth-generation total information system
- Installed satellite antennas
- New POS registers introduced
- Ticket sales using multi-functional copier

Distribution System Innovation

- Reduced number of vendors
- Started twice-a-day deliveries of rice products
- Started combined distribution of dairy products
- Started combined distribution of frozen foods
- Started combined distribution of refrigerated foods
- Started three-times-a-day deliveries of rice products
- Self-confirmation system expanded
- Started frozen-food warehouse system for combined distribution
- Started three-times-a-day combined distribution of refrigerated items
- Introduced a weather information system
- Combined distribution of rice products and chilled items
- Started combined distribution of nonfood items
- Seven-Meal Service

Note: EOS (electronic ordering system), EOB (electronic order book), ST (scanner terminal), SC (store computer), ISDN (integrated services digital network).

Source: 7-Eleven Japan. Used with permission.

One of SEJ's earliest distribution management initiatives was to combine similar products from different suppliers at a delivery center. By first combining dairy products, then frozen products, then refrigerated products, and later rice and fresh food products and nonfood items, SEJ reduced the number of different deliveries a store received each day from seventy to nine over an eighteen-year period. SEJ's manufacturers now deliver to one of four "combined delivery centers," which, in turn, ship to the stores in four types of vans classified by the temperature of the goods: frozen, chilled, room temperature, and hot.

By the early eighties SEJ was introducing technology support for inventory and distribution management, including its first point-of-sale (POS) systems. The POS data helped SEJ analyze its customers' buying habits to improve the product ordering process. The POS data became even more valuable in the early nineties when SEJ installed high-speed telecommunications lines and subsequently satellite antennae. High-speed telecommunications provide instantaneous sales reports to SEJ's entire supply chain.

Today SEJ's "total information system" connects 70,000 computers in stores, at headquarters, and at supplier sites, providing transparency across the entire value chain.[5] Vendors, distributors, and manufacturers share a common infrastructure consisting of 1,800 terminals at 1,100 locations. The standardized systems handle raw material ordering, inventory management, production management, and automated sorting. SEJ's partners are delighted with the information, as a salesperson for one supplier commented: "Their information system is so good that we can now instantly find out which goods of ours are selling and how much."[6]

Meanwhile, store employees can access recent sales, weather conditions, and product information, all presented graphically, to support store orders. SEJ trains store owners and clerks, including part-time workers, in inventory management. In addition, counselors visit stores twice a week to provide advice on store operations and information on the portfolio of available items. The professional development of even part-time employees allows stores to benefit from SEJ's practice of ordering and delivering fresh food three times a day. The result is that on hot days Tokyo's 7-Eleven stores have plenty of bento boxes while on cold days there are lots of hot noodles for sale.

Seven-Eleven Japan's digitized distribution and inventory management capabilities give it agility with product mix. The result is an industry-leading 70 percent of each store's products being new each year. Because all SEJ employees rigidly follow standardized processes for identifying and ordering the products their store's customers most want, SEJ achieves customer loyalty and higher sales. SEJ's foundation for execution helped SEJ stores to nearly double the average daily sales between 1977 and 1992. Seven-Eleven Japan's average daily sales are 35 percent higher than industry average.

Profitable Growth in a Coordination Model

In a Coordination operating model, a company leverages a strong IT infrastructure to share data across unique businesses. As a company matures its architecture, the foundation of shared, easily accessible data becomes increasingly powerful. Profitable growth comes from superior customer service, better knowledge of customer buying patterns and needs, and greater ability to cross-sell and upsell customers. This improved understanding of customers leads to better business decisions and better-targeted new products. New products and services come from business units that are not bound by standard processes—which encourages local innovation. MetLife is a good example of a company leveraging its foundation to provide a growing set of products to a growing set of customers.

MetLife, formed in 1863, is the United States' largest life insurer.[7] MetLife's chairman and CEO, Robert Benmosche, defines the company's mission as "to build financial freedom for everyone." To achieve that vision, MetLife needs to create an ever-growing portfolio of financial products. MetLife is working to provide an integrated view of its products for its customers and a single view of the customer for its employees to enable better service.

Like most financial services companies, MetLife's history works against integration. In the past twenty years, MetLife has undergone a series of mergers, so its systems legacy includes systems from several large, formerly independent companies. MetLife has been structured by product line, where systems were built to sell one product to many customers and not to provide an integrated view of customers. Adding to the complexity of MetLife's systems and processes, the company sells directly to individuals as well as through employers who provide MetLife products as an employee benefit.

To integrate data, Executive Vice President and CIO Steven Sheinheit focuses on clarifying what data is needed and how it is created. While some Coordination companies look to packaged customer relationship management systems to provide integration, MetLife's large-scale and complex relationships cannot be easily addressed by packaged software. Instead, the company relies on world-class technical talent to provide the integration of packaged software with the needed infrastructure, as well as to design the information architecture and extract the needed data.

Integrated customer data enables MetLife employees to understand their customers, follow the history of transactions, and provide better service. MetLife's "One MetLife" initiative, to attack the inefficiencies of its history of product line structures and growth by acquisition, will introduce greater business process standardization throughout the company. However, the thrust of its enterprise architecture is business integration enabled by shared data access. Data access is what MetLife people need to meet customer needs and sell company products. Because employees need not spend time tracking down data to answer customer questions or resolve issues, more of MetLife's resources can go into developing new products that help customers "build financial freedom." In 2004 MetLife added products like critical-illness insurance, a suite of retirement products designed to provide "income for life," and an innovative survivor income benefit for its universal life product.

Business units in a Coordination model have considerable autonomy in designing products and serving customers. This autonomy encourages product innovation and allows companies to expand revenue per customer while also appealing to a broader range of customers. Building and leveraging its foundation through new products, MetLife generated record net income in 2002, 2003, and 2004.

Profitable Growth in a Diversification Model

In a Diversification operating model, there may be no integration or standardization of business processes across business units. Companies grow by giving business units autonomy to pursue local growth, or they create or acquire new businesses. As a Diversification company matures its enterprise architecture, it offers shared IT infrastructure to reduce costs across the company. Many Diversification companies will not mature their architecture past stage 2, wishing only to generate some economies of scale in IT. Those that move to stage 3 focus on introducing shared services for functions like finance, HR, and purchasing.

Diversification companies choosing not to mature their architecture rely on management capability (e.g., risk management, merger and acquisition capability, etc.) to add shareholder value from headquarters. This model of a diversified company, typified by GE and Johnson & Johnson through the 1980s, has largely lost favor among stockholders. More often, companies with a Diversification model choose to hold a portfolio of businesses with a natural synergy and thus have some corporate technical standards and shared services.

For example, Carlson Companies has a portfolio of brands in the hospitality industry. While hotels, restaurants, cruise ships, and travel agencies don't share many business processes, they do have natural synergies. So Carlson has been able to generate economies from shared infrastructure and shared services, particularly finance. The company also anticipates developing a data store to leverage multiple relationships with customers. Diversification companies don't need an extensive foundation for execution company-wide, but they can take a few relatively simple actions that generate cost savings and cross-business-unit synergies.

Managing the Architecture Through Mergers and Acquisitions

Acquisitions are easiest, though arguably least valuable, in companies with a Diversification model. Diversification demands minimal organizational change. In the other three models, the challenge of growing by acquisition rather than organically is that two companies have to try to merge incompatible foundations. If the two companies involved in an acquisition have not achieved the same stage of architecture maturity, the change can be highly disruptive. For example, if a company with a stage 3 enterprise architecture acquires a company with a stage 1 enterprise architecture, the acquiring company can install its foundation, but the acquired company will have to skip stages. As we noted earlier in the book, skipping stages imposes significant learning requirements on a company. During the learning process, the acquiring company may regress to stage 1 or stage 2 by virtue of its acquisition.

Even if two companies are at the same architectural stage, a merger will be disruptive as management sorts out which of the two foundations for execution will work best. Some companies try to pick and choose from the two companies' best capabilities. But if the companies have not achieved modularity in their business design, such selectivity will almost certainly cause problems. Nonetheless, some companies outside the Diversification quadrant have the agility to grow profitably through mergers and acquisitions. We have observed two different architectural approaches to profitable growth through acquisitions:

1. The company leverages a mature foundation either through a strategy of ripping out existing processes at the acquired company and installing the digitized processes of the acquiring company (Unification or Replication), or through a strategy of moving the acquisition onto a standard portal and forcing data integration (Coordination).

2. The company makes the acquisition for purposes of market synergies and does not attempt to integrate or standardize the new business, thus moving the enterprise as a whole to a Diversification operating model.

CEMEX provides an example of the rip-and-replace strategy. UPS's recent growth illustrates the diversification strategy.

The Acquisition Process at CEMEX: Rip and Replace

CEMEX, a $7 billion Mexican cement manufacturer, has long been admired for its IT capabilities relative to its competitors.[8] As early as 1987, the company built telecommunications capabilities to coordinate the activities of its production facilities and later to support dispatching of ready-made concrete. In 1990 CEMEX developed an executive information system that focused IT capabilities on providing access to operating information—this system also forced business managers to think about how to use information to improve operating results. In 1992 CEMEX implemented an ERP system, applying IT to standardize processes like finance and distribution. These capabilities have helped CEMEX grow from Mexico's second-largest cement producer in 1990 (tenth in the world) to the world's third-largest cement producer in 2003. Of the world's top three cement companies, CEMEX has the highest profit margin and highest net sales and cash flow per employee.

In the early 1990s, Lorenzo Zambrano, CEMEX's CEO and grandson of its founder, recognized that CEMEX could not escape the impacts of global competition. He said, "We suddenly found ourselves competing with very large international companies at a time of consolidation in the global cement industry. There were few independent producers left. Either we became large and international, or we would end up being purchased by a bigger player."[9]

Zambrano responded to this threat by purchasing Spain's two largest cement producers in 1992. Subsequently, CEMEX acquired companies in thirty countries, including the United States, Japan, France, Panama, the Dominican Republic, Indonesia, and the Philippines. CEMEX sent postmerger acquisition teams to the acquired companies to facilitate integration and knowledge transfer. In early acquisitions, teams spent as long as twenty-four months training managers on CEMEX practices. Despite initial resistance from local managers, the implementation of the CEMEX foundation led to significant improvements in the operating results of its acquisitions. Companies acquired between 1992 and 1996 increased their operating margins by an average of more than 10 percent in the three years after acquisition.

Despite Cemex's efforts to share management practices, the acquisitions led to a proliferation of systems and processes and climbing IT costs. Zambrano believed the solution was to standardize best practices globally: "The company now is much more complex, and we had to go through a process of amalgamating our business processes throughout the world, saying, 'This is THE CEMEX WAY of doing x, y, and z' . . . and it became a way of growing very fast and leveraging what we know."[10]

Building on earlier efforts to increase process standardization, Zambrano launched the "CEMEX Way" in 2000. This initiative standardized eight key business processes: commercial (customer facing and cement logistics), ready-mix manufacturing, accounting, planning and budgeting, operations, procurement, finance, and HR. In 2004 he created the IT and business process evolution organization, which looked for additional opportunities to leverage IT not only for business process standardization but also for local innovation and global sharing of best practices.

The company's focus on IT-enabled process standardization and process improvement has facilitated assimilation of its acquisitions. For example, in 2000 CEMEX acquired Southland, the United States' second-largest cement manufacturer, in a $2.8 billion deal. IT and process teams completed assimilation in four months. Subsequent acquisitions have been assimilated in as little as two months.[11]

CEMEX's biggest challenge in acquisitions is to bring the learning of a stage 3 architecture to the new company. CEMEX's former head of information technology described the challenge this way: "The biggest stumbling block lies with people. When you make a foreign acquisition you face biases and reluctance to give up current practices and corporate cultures. While the importance of platforms is undeniable, technology is not an end in itself. Management must figure out how its processes, functions and systems can accommodate the different needs of the employees."[12]

CEMEX rapidly replaces existing technology platforms and business processes in the companies it acquires. Such rip-and-replace efforts, however, meet with resistance from the acquired company's employees. CEMEX invests heavily in training—sending in teams of strong managers who work with the new company's management team. With strong performance results and appropriate rewards, the resistance subsides and enthusiasm builds. We do not know of an alternative approach that allows a company to avoid slipping back to a less mature architecture following an acquisition.

The Acquisition Process at UPS: Moving to a Diversification Model

UPS has created opportunities for growth by adding new businesses that, while becoming profitable in their own right, are expected to add value by feeding the core. Much like Schneider National's transition to a Diversification model as it developed a logistics business (see chapter 2), UPS builds and acquires businesses related to package delivery. These new businesses cannot use the existing foundation for execution for new business operations because they operate differently.

With its package delivery business at its core, UPS has crafted a set of smaller, growth-oriented businesses such as UPS Supply Chain Solutions, UPS Capital Corp., UPS Consulting, The UPS Store/Mail Boxes Etc., and UPS Professional Services (figure 8-2). CEO Mike Eskew explains the rationale for the new businesses: "The core package business has a lot of growth opportunities and capability . . . but we also need to sow new areas that leverage on that core. Some of those new areas will fail . . . and we would like them to fail fast. And some of them will work . . . As much as we can, we will integrate that [new business] into the core. We are seeing terrific opportunities in logistics with Capital Corp. . . . and our service parts businesses. We are going to find new ways to expand this core business by trying new things and feed that core."[13]

Unlike UPS's core business expansion into the global business arena, its new businesses do not leverage UPS's economies of scale or foundation for execution. UPS can certainly leverage its industrial-engineering expertise and elements of its core IT infrastructure in new businesses. But the invaluable standard package delivery processes that give UPS so much agility in its core business don't provide much value to its new businesses. Laurie Johnson, CIO of UPS Supply Chain Solutions, explains the boundaries between the core business and UPS's newer subsidiaries: "I'd love to leverage what's good about the core, but the subsidiaries still need a different sense of urgency; the ability to take higher risks with products, technologies, and customer relationships; flexibility that allows us to serve the customer faster, better, cheaper— and rules that are made to be broken."[14]

These new businesses don't leverage UPS's foundation for execution, but they feed the core business by increasing package volumes, which creates strong market synergies and a very profitable,

FIGURE 8-2

The UPS business model

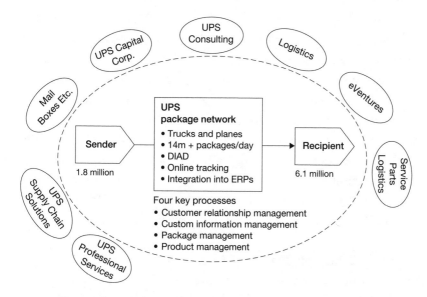

Note: UPS Professional Services and UPS Consulting fall under the UPS Supply Chain Solutions umbrella in the enterprisewide structure.

Source: Derived from (1) Jeanne W. Ross, "United Parcel Service: Delivering Packages and E-Commerce Solutions," working paper 318, MIT Sloan Center for Information Systems Research, Cambridge, MA, August 2001, and (2) Peter Weill and Michael R. Vitale, *Place to Space: Migrating to eBusiness Models* (Boston: Harvard Business School Press, 2001).

self-reinforcing business model. UPS is developing a parallel foundation to support the new businesses.

The Acquisition Process at 7-Eleven Japan: Moving Toward Modularity

7-Eleven Japan has achieved much of its growth through a rip-and-replace approach to acquiring new stores. Although management believes the company still has many opportunities to grow in Japan, SEJ is looking for additional growth opportunities. Like UPS, it adopts some diversification practices to extend its range of opportunities.

Recently, SEJ purchased a controlling interest in 7-Eleven Inc. Expanding into the U.S. market creates new challenges. The market share of convenience stores is much lower in the United States, where the market is heterogeneous, the income gap is bigger, and the shopper is more cost sensitive than in Japan. In addition, unlike the Japanese stores that became franchisees one at a time, the United States already has almost 6,000 stores. James Keyes, president and CEO of 7-Eleven Inc., believes SEJ will succeed in bringing value to the U.S. market: "7-Eleven of the United States will have a strong potential for success if we learn more about 7-Eleven Japan's item-by-item control and effective delivery system."[15]

Facing different demographics and an established base of stores, SEJ may not be able to simply rip and replace the foundation in 6,000 U.S. stores. Instead, it may have to pick and choose modules that will work in the United States. This will demand increased modularity—a stage 4 level of architecture maturity.

What's Next? The Fifth Stage of Architecture Maturity

As companies achieve stage 4 architecture maturity, they might like to stop and rest. But we doubt that Business Modularity is the last stage. Thomas Jefferson once remarked, "I like the dreams of the future better than the history of the past."[16] In the spirit of Jefferson, we will now set aside some of the legacy of the past and present our view of the next stage of maturity.

We call the fifth stage of architecture maturity "Dynamic Venturing." Building naturally on the capabilities developed in the Business Modularity stage, the fifth stage extends the concept of reusable modules to enable companies to rapidly reconfigure their portfolios of businesses. Based on the core capabilities of the company, managers will look for opportunities to partner, acquire, joint-venture, collaborate, integrate, and connect with many other companies. Business strategies will focus on dynamically coupling with many other businesses to quickly exploit market opportunities by bringing together the world's best players at each position in the value chain.

The Dow Chemical Vision of Stage 5

Dow Chemical's Federated Broker Model, described earlier in the book, offers one glimpse of the fifth stage.[17] Dave Kepler, corporate vice president for shared services and CIO, explains Dow's vision:

> Historically, the JVs [joint ventures] we've managed stand alone or Dow had a responsibility for the operational management and the other partner didn't put a lot of their own employees in. The JVs we're going into now—in the Middle East and China—are not going to be as highly leveraged and integrated into the company's business model, but have a mix of companies and employees engaged. So, we know our systems need to be more flexible to support this model. We need to leverage Dow's know-how and low cost structure, and we have to put some [IT] architecture in to give the JV the capability that we've negotiated, but not at the expense of opening up our entire enterprise.

Kepler is already facing the need for a stage 5 architecture, but Dow will learn how to build stage 5 capabilities as it works its way through stage 4. In stage 4 Dow will increasingly plug and play process modules. In the fifth stage, a company can plug and play new businesses, not just process modules.

Characterizing a Stage 5 Company

In stage 5, business components will be both self-contained and readily connectable. The kinds of industry-standard software interfaces and intelligent agents emerging now will be critical to this stage. The standard interfaces will allow components from virtually any company to dynamically couple with any other company—of course, with the appropriate informed consent and protection! Intelligent agents will help by seeking out opportunities, negotiating prices, and brokering deals automatically within predetermined limits. Table 8-1 extends table 4-1 to show the key characteristics of the fifth stage as compared to earlier stages.

In the fifth stage companies will give business partners selective access to their key data and business processes. Early forays toward this goal include UPS's embedding its software into large ERP systems. As a result of these partnerships, customers of the major ERP vendors have a direct electronic link via the purchasing module of their ERP system into UPS's Web site, providing logistics and tracking capabilities. IBM—by opening up more of its research capability to customers—is moving toward the goal of reconfigurable businesses. Amazon's Marketplace for hard-to-find books and other items dynamically links thousands of third-party sellers with millions of buyers. Customers prespecify the items, condition, and price they are willing to pay, and Amazon Marketplace makes matches. These efforts are not Dynamic Venturing, but they are harbingers of business capability to come.

In the fifth stage business components will be based on the unique intellectual property of the owner and have at least the following elements:

- *Business rules:* how to conduct the business of the component

- *Business process:* optimized business process steps exposed to potential partners

TABLE 8-1

Learning requirements of all five architecture stages

	Business Silos	Standardized Technology	Optimized Core	Business Modularity	Dynamic Venturing
IT capability	Local IT applications	Shared technical platforms	Companywide standardized processes or databases	Plug-and-play business process modules	Seamless merging with partners' systems
Business objectives	ROI of local business initiatives	Reduced IT costs	Cost and quality of business operations	Speed to market; strategic agility	ROI of new business ventures
Key management capability	Technology-enabled change management	Design and update of standards; funding shared services	Core enterprise process definition and measurement	Management of reusable business processes	Create self-contained business components
Who defines applications	Local business leaders	IT and business unit leaders	Senior management and process leaders	IT, business, and industry leaders	IT, business, and industry leaders and partners
Key IT governance issues	Measuring and communicating value	Establishing local/regional/global responsibilities	Aligning project priorities with architecture objectives	Defining, sourcing, and funding business modules	Joint venture governance
Strategic implications	Local/functional optimization	IT efficiency	Business/operational efficiency	Strategic agility	Organic reconfiguration

© 2005 MIT Sloan Center for Information Systems Research and IMD. Used with permission.

- *Data:* key data to be shared and data to be kept private for competitive or legal reasons, accessible through standard modular interfaces

- *Interfaces:* standardized ways to connect to the components of many other partners, including customers, governments, joint ventures, vendors, outsourcers, service providers, and regulators

- *Security:* rules for connecting, encryption, self-diagnostics, defense against attacks, and the like

- *Rules for coupling:* strategic, negotiated, and legal rules embedded into the component

Preparing for Stage 5

Few companies are ready to think specifically about how they will adapt to the fifth stage. But, like prior stages, the fifth stage will be a natural evolution from the modularity of the fourth stage. Clearly, there are many strategic, legal, technical, financial, risk, and other issues to be addressed. We are convinced, however, that the concept of a portfolio of businesses that dynamically couple—based on their unique capabilities captured in components—is the logical extension of the economic and business conditions we face today.

In the immediate future, we recommend that your company focus on squeezing all the value you can out of your current stage of architecture maturity. In doing so, you will position your company for the next stage—and all the benefits associated with it. Just as we argue against big-bang implementations of enterprise architecture capabilities, we caution you not to expect big-bang benefits. But we do believe that as you build your foundation for execution, you will build a much stronger performing company, one that regularly discovers happy surprises. Thinking about what dynamic coupling means in your company will help set your long-term architecture goals and identify the business modules needed in stage 4.

9

Take Charge!
The Leadership Agenda

Why not upset the apple cart.
If you don't, the apples will rot anyway.

—Frank A. Clark[1]

IN CHAPTER 1 we described the benefits of a foundation for execution. Now we ask—would you like your business to have:

- Higher profitability?

- Faster time to market?

- More value from your IT investments?

- Twenty-five percent lower IT costs?

- Better access to shared customer data?

- Lower risk of mission-critical systems failures?

- Eighty percent higher senior management satisfaction with technology?

To achieve these objectives via a foundation for execution there is one more question to answer: what is the leadership agenda for creating and leveraging a foundation for execution?

Throughout this book we have argued for upsetting the apple cart—rethinking how your company builds and leverages capabilities. This chapter lays out a leadership agenda. First, we consider the case for action in your company. We look at nine symptoms of an ineffective foundation for execution—the more symptoms like these you see, the more urgent the need for senior management action. Then we briefly review the steps to designing or rethinking your foundation for execution and acquiring key organizational learning. Finally, we identify the top ten leadership principles for building and exploiting your foundation.

Symptoms of an Ineffective Foundation for Execution

In chapter 1 we provided a substantial list of the warning signs of not having a foundation for execution to support strategy. We suggested you would find this book helpful if one or more of the warning signs were true of your organization. Now we will explore some of these warning signs in more detail, identifying symptoms of problems and metrics for you to self-assess. The objective is to help you calibrate the urgency of your company's need to work on its foundation for execution.

One Customer Question Elicits Different Answers

When customers get different answers to the same question from different parts of your company, two bad things happen. First, the customer gets annoyed and confused. This was exactly the experience Delta Air Lines had when employees could not accurately answer a question about the time a flight was expected. Second, people in your organization have to do loads of rework to fix the problem. At Delta the result was that employees were frustrated because they didn't have the tools to do their job—the confrontations between frustrated customers and poorly equipped employees were neither pleasant nor productive. And then someone would have to follow up with the correct information. Before Delta invested in its Delta nervous system (see chapter 3) employees were looking at different systems that used different and sometimes conflicting data—there was no foundation for execution. Actually, there were *several* incompatible functional foundations!

Think back over the past year in a customer-facing group you know well and ask yourself what percentage of employees' total time was spent on rework—that is, redoing something that should have been done right the first time. Ideally, the answer is zero. The higher the percentage in your company, the more urgent the case for action.

New Regulations Require Major Effort

For some companies listed on stock exchanges in the United States, Sarbanes-Oxley was a motivation to create a better foundation for execution that also included meeting the government's new reporting requirements. For many other companies, it was yet another mandatory investment diverting resources from important business initiatives. A *CIO Magazine* tech poll reports that nearly half of the large companies surveyed will divert more than 15 percent of their 2005 IT budgets to Sarbanes-Oxley compliance.[2] In sharing this figure with an audience of CIOs, Gary Beach, publisher of *CIO Magazine,* was met by a sea of heads nodding in disgust. Afterward, a CIO said to him, "I make a lot of sales calls and never once have I heard a sales rep tout to a prospective customer: the reason you should do business with us is because we are more compliant than our competition."

Regulatory compliance creates overhead, but new regulations will likely appear every year. A foundation for execution significantly reduces the marginal cost of meeting the next regulation by creating a reusable capability to access data and metrics. In your organization what percentage of the IT budget is allocated to meeting regulatory requirements (often called "mandatory investment")? If that percentage doesn't decrease over time, and especially if it's anywhere near 15 percent, your case for action is urgent.[3]

Business Agility Is Difficult and Growth Initiatives Aren't Profitable

It takes time to develop new capabilities. Thus, when a growth initiative forces a company to develop new capabilities, the initiative is usually slow to yield a profit. For example, mergers and acquisitions—such as Time Warner–AOL and Chase Manhattan–JPMorgan—are often slow to deliver expected economies because they fail to leverage an existing foundation. Similarly, new market initiatives, such as AT&T's early foray into television or GM's pioneering efforts with OnStar, are typically better at generating revenues than profits.

In our research, companies with a higher percentage of their core business processes digitized were more agile.[4] In contrast, companies that were not building and leveraging digitized capabilities felt as if they were starting over to develop new capabilities to address each new management directive. Do your new strategic initiatives leverage existing capabilities? One useful metric for agility is the percentage of your company's revenues that comes from new products introduced in the past three years.

In chapter 1 we reported that for companies in our research, the percentage of sales from new products introduced in the past three years was 24 percent.[5] This type of agility varied greatly by company even in the same industry. For example, in manufacturing the average was also 24 percent. However, a third of manufacturing companies were much more agile, achieving 50 percent of sales from new products introduced in the past three years. The least agile third of companies only achieved 5 percent of sales from new products. A foundation for execution makes a big difference.

How agile is your firm? What percentage of last year's sales came from new products introduced in the past three years? How profitable are your new initiatives? How urgent is the case for action?

IT Is Consistently a Bottleneck

Companies pursuing IT implementations the old-fashioned way (i.e., by articulating business strategy and then aligning IT) usually find that IT is a bottleneck rather than a strategic asset. In many companies the standard answer to a question about how long it will take to implement a new system to support a new strategic initiative is one to two years. During that time the market and the business will change. In contrast, Citibank Asia starts up services in new regions faster than the competition using a preexisting credit-card-processing capability tailored for local needs. And UPS regularly introduces new customer services based on existing customer and package information. Top companies are increasingly demanding that projects deliver added value every ninety days.

By focusing IT investments on enabling the integration and standardization required of the company's operating model, a company prepares itself for future strategic initiatives, without knowing what those initiatives might be. What is your average lead time for new initiatives? If your large projects don't consistently deliver value in fewer than twelve months, the case for action is urgent.

Different Business Processes and Systems Complete the Same Activity

One large, global manufacturing company we visited had twenty-nine order-entry systems. A large insurance company had more than thirty different ways to pay customer benefits. A pharmaceutical company had eighteen inventory management systems. And another insurance company had more than twenty underwriting systems. The IT departments in these companies operated these systems, enhanced functionality when requested, and maintained the technical platform supporting each individual system. Redundant systems are expensive. In addition, they are difficult to integrate with other systems, so companies run the risk of inaccurate data for compliance reporting, customer service, and management decision making. Sometimes, real business differences justify the existence of different systems supporting the same process; the expense of implementing common systems and processes does not outweigh the benefits. But many companies are paying excessively for variation that doesn't add value—and might very well undermine a foundation for execution.

How many different business processes and associated systems exist in your company to complete the same activity? Are they adding value? If the number of redundant systems in your company isn't declining, the case for action is urgent.

Information Necessary for Making Decisions Is Not Available

7-Eleven Japan stores manage thrice-daily orders for same-day delivery based on current sales, weather, and inventory levels (see chapter 8). Marriott prices rooms based on up-to-the-minute demand forecasting information.[6] But many companies still rely on approximations and instinct to make key operating decisions. Companies have spent enormous sums developing data warehouses, implementing customer relationship management systems, and installing middleware to provide better data access. But these investments haven't necessarily led to better decisions—either the right information isn't available, or the decision maker doesn't know how to use it effectively.

A strong foundation for execution has the data decision makers need. People know how to use the data to make decisions, often by enacting standardized processes. Do your decision makers take effective action on the same set of useful customer and product data every day? If not, your case for action is urgent.

Employees Move Data from One System to Another

When people key in data from one system to another, they are doing work computers do better. Worse, the process introduces opportunity for errors, and a company's scarcest resource—attention—is being wasted. Financial services companies have long valued straight-through processing of key business processes. *Straight-through processing* refers to business processes, such as buying or selling a security, that are being completed without humans processing the data. The concept of straight-through processing can be applied to any industry—many retail stores and service providers have automated replenishment systems to reorder everyday items. For example, HP offers auto-replenishment where printers automatically reorder cartridges when toner runs low, without user intervention and within certain preset limits.[7]

On average, companies complete 19 percent of their sales and 23 percent of their purchases electronically with little variation across industries.[8] However, the third of companies with the most digitized processes complete 50 percent of their sales and 55 percent of their purchases electronically. How do you compare? What percentage of your key transactional processes requires people to take data from one system, manipulate it, and enter it into another system? If that percentage is above zero and isn't consistently decreasing, your case for action is urgent.

Senior Management Dreads Discussing IT Agenda Items

A key mechanism in most companies' IT governance is the senior executive committee that deals with IT. These committees are critical to establishing IT principles and priorities for IT investment.

Despite this important role, many senior executives dread IT steering committee meetings—one executive described them to us as "mind-numbingly boring." In some companies, it is not uncommon for senior executives to send a staffer to meetings in their place.

When senior executives are not engaged in IT decision making, they cannot provide direction or incentives for the company to build and exploit a valuable foundation for execution. Without senior management involvement the IT unit takes on too much risk—and is actually best off spending as little as possible.

The CIO of the average company rates the success of his or her most senior committee as 3.5 (on a scale of 1 to 5). In top-performing companies CIOs rate these committees at 4.1 (on a scale of 1 to 5).[9] CIOs of these effective committees set agendas that focus their senior management colleagues on strategic issues and choices. The project reviews and detailed technical matters are handled elsewhere. How effective is the most senior committee that makes your IT decisions? If that score is less than 3.5, your case for action is urgent.

Management Doesn't Know Whether It Gets Good Value from IT

If senior executives don't know whether they are getting good value from IT, it's a sure bet they aren't. As companies build IT capabilities, either they exploit those capabilities in ways that are both visible and measurable, or they are wasting money. Recently, as the CIO of a large financial services company sat in a meeting, he received the following message on his BlackBerry from his CEO: "How does the [XYZ] project affect our enterprise architecture?" If it's never occurred to you to ponder that question, you are part of the problem, not part of the solution.

As noted in chapter 5, companies getting strategic value from IT have senior managers specifying requirements for enterprise architecture and overseeing the results of architecture initiatives (table 5-1). These senior managers are also more likely to be able to describe the company's high-level enterprise architecture. What percentage of senior managers at your company can describe, at a high level, your enterprise architecture? If the answer is less than a third, your case for action is urgent.

Looking back over your answers to the questions about symptoms, how urgent is the case for action in your company? If your company reaches the threshold described on any one symptom (e.g., less than a third of senior managers can describe enterprise architecture) your business process and IT capabilities are undermining, rather than contributing to, your competitiveness. The more symptoms observed (relative to the thresholds) in a company, the sicker the foundation and the more urgent the need for management attention. The next section presents a brief summary of the steps to attack the symptoms by designing or rethinking your foundation for execution (the chapter in parentheses provides details).

Key Steps in Rethinking Your Foundation for Execution

We advocate six steps to rethink your foundation for execution:

1. Analyze your existing foundation for execution (chapter 1).

2. Define your operating model (chapter 2)

3. Design your enterprise architecture (chapters 3 and 4).

4. Set priorities (chapters 4 and 5).

5. Design and implement an IT engagement model (chapter 6).

6. Exploit your foundation for execution for growth (chapter 8).

These steps should be a group exercise for members of the senior management team. To be valuable the first four steps should be intense, even confrontational, exercises between senior executives. If everyone quickly agrees, management hasn't recognized that these steps set the direction for the company—how the company will grow, what projects you'll pursue, how IT investment dollars will be spent. If you don't force a shared understanding of your operating model and enterprise architecture, you will fritter away your company's resources on projects that don't matter, and you will watch more-focused companies march off with your customers.

Step 1: Analyze Your Existing Foundation for Execution

Examine figures 1-3 and 1-4. These are abbreviated analyses of the foundations for execution at UPS and the government of the District of Columbia. Using the generic form of this assessment (figure 1-2), consider each element in your foundation for execution. Questions to consider include the following:

- What processes are digitized end-to-end? Are these mission-critical transactions in your company?

- What data is easily accessible to your employees and customers? Is this the data they most need to make decisions leading to customer and shareholder value?

- What elements of IT infrastructure are world class?

- Does the infrastructure provide the reach, security, data access, and flexibility you need?

- What strengths and weaknesses do you see in your foundation?

Step 2: Define Your Operating Model

Your operating model should encapsulate your integration and standardization requirements. To design your operating model, complete the following exercises:

- *Identify the processes that distinguish you competitively.* Determine what elements of those processes should be standardized across the company.

- *Envision your customer's experience as it ought to be.* Determine what integration of data and end-to-end connection of processes is necessary to make that real.

- *Decide how you would like your company to grow.* Can you offer current customers more products or services? Should you expand globally? Should you acquire competitors? Should you acquire or grow adjacent businesses?

Once you have articulated your expectations, examine figures 2-1 and 2-3 to determine which operating model best meets your requirements. The good (and bad) news is that you only have four options to choose from. Pick one dominant model at each level in your company to provide a clear vision of how the company will operate.

Step 3: Design Your Enterprise Architecture

Once you have defined how you want to operate and grow, you are ready to rough out your core companywide business processes, shared data, key technologies, and critical customer interfaces. Start by using the process and operating model templates from chapter 3 as a guide. For example, if your base operating model is Unification, figure 3-2 identifies three elements that must be part of your foundation for execution: customer interfaces, processes, and data. Apply the appropriate template (figure 3-2, 3-4, 3-6, or 3-8) for your operating model.

If you find you have too many elements to fit onto one standard-sized piece of paper, take your discussion up a level. You're not trying to identify every important process, data element, or technology. The key is to recognize which particular elements compose the essence of your business—your foundation for execution.

Step 4: Set Priorities

Most organizations have more change initiatives than they can reasonably implement. The enterprise architecture core diagram reveals a company's priorities because it highlights the base on which future capabilities depend. Building out the foundation for execution demands management focus, particularly at budget time. A company's project portfolio should reflect its enterprise architecture priorities.

We suggest that every major project champion in the company should address the following question: how can the project build out or leverage the foundation for execution?

If the answer is that the project can't, the company should investigate carefully whether the project has strategic value. Urgent business needs might require that some projects not help push the architecture forward. But, for the most part, the company should leverage project-related expenditures to help evolve and improve the foundation for execution.

Step 5: Design and Implement an IT Engagement Model

To sustain focus on iteratively building and leveraging a foundation for execution, companies need a formal IT engagement model. As described in chapter 6, three ingredients are critical: (1) IT governance at the senior levels of the company, (2) disciplined project management across all major projects, and (3) linkages to ensure that IT governance and project management mutually reinforce one another.

All three of these ingredients require management to implement mechanisms for articulating company goals, setting priorities, managing to objectives, and measuring results. The engagement model brings continuous reinforcement of company goals in everyday tasks, making it a critical tool for building and leveraging a foundation for execution.

Step 6: Exploit Your Foundation for Growth

Even as you start building the foundation you must cash in on the benefits. This means first allocating generous funding for training and development. If the company's people don't know how to use the foundation, the payback won't happen. Second, align incentives so that people are motivated to exploit the foundation. If the operating model demands integration and standardization, make sure reward systems encourage integration and standardization, not individual heroics. Third, encourage and reward creativity. Creativity identifies—both from the outside in and the inside out—opportunities for new and existing products and markets. Outside-in creativity looks to the marketplace to identify opportunities that leverage or add to the foundation. Inside-out creativity looks to the foundation to see what is possible and may appeal to customers. As the company learns how to effectively deploy the foundation—particularly via testimonials of successful initiatives—everyone will become clearer about the benefits of the foundation.

Top Ten Leadership Principles

From studying and working with hundreds of companies, we have distilled lessons from many outstanding executives into ten leadership principles for creating and exploiting a foundation for execution. We intend these to provide a succinct summary of the book and a primer, refresher, or checklist for all leaders.[10]

1. Commit to the Foundation

A foundation for execution should have fundamental impacts on how a company does business. Instead of strategies based on reacting to customer demands and competitor initiatives, a company with a foundation will primarily base its strategies on identifying opportunities to leverage its capabilities. Management literature has long preached that companies must develop and apply unique capabilities to succeed in global markets.[11] The foundation-for-execution framework provides an orderly view of how to plan, implement, and leverage a coherent set of capabilities.

Companies must exercise strong organizational discipline to build and leverage a foundation. First, a company must embrace the discipline to declare an operating model and implement the required standardization of processes, data, and technology. Second, management must embrace the discipline to pursue those strategic opportunities that leverage its foundation—without forcing opportunities that don't fit. As ING DIRECT (chapter 3) follows its established formula for success, introducing a narrow set of existing products into new banks in new countries, it is bucking the trend toward full-service financial institutions. Its success reflects discipline in both its business processes and its strategic decisions.

2. Initiate Change from the Top and Remove Barriers

Building a foundation for execution is central to a company's ability to execute its strategies and thus needs the attention and dedication of senior management. Left to their own devices, most people in a company attempt to do what they think is right. But without clear direction, some of their actions will do as much harm as good. Senior management needs to drive the choice of the operating model and be involved in the articulation of the enterprise architecture. And senior managers should take responsibility for converting an architecture into a foundation for execution both directly and via reinforcing governance.

The need for senior management leadership and funding is visible in the leader-follower dilemma. Building out the foundation for execution requires investments in IT infrastructure, but as companies build out their foundations one project at a time, funding mechanisms often limit important investments in infrastructure. For example, the securities trading business unit in a financial services company with multiple business units was the first to identify a valuable customer service using wireless tech-nologies. The company's funding mechanisms required the inno-vating business unit to pay for the entire wireless infrastructure, even though other parts of the company had identified wireless technologies as important to their future. Faced with paying the full infrastructure cost, the business unit leader was motivated to create a silo of technology because an enterprisewide solution would cost more and take longer to integrate into the foundation. There are many solutions to this dilemma. For example, corporate can underwrite a percentage of the cost of the infrastructure. Al-ternatively, or in addition, the business leading the investment can receive a dividend from business unit followers as a reward for taking the lead and the risk. In any case, senior management can-not simply decide how the company will operate—it must rectify all the forces working against its vision. Senior management must create the climate for success.

3. Feed the Core—Experiment

While companies are pursuing profitable growth by building and leveraging a foundation for execution, they will certainly encounter promising strategic opportunities that don't leverage their foun-dation. When market synergies argue for strategic bets that can-not leverage an existing foundation, companies should pursue them separately from the core business, as Schneider National's logistics business, UPS's financial services business, and Manheim's online auctions all did. Such ventures allow a company to experiment with synergistic businesses that might feed the core.

A strong foundation for execution prepares the company for unknown future customer demands. A stream of small, focused experiments apart from the core helps a company learn about emerging businesses and the capabilities of new technologies. Be-cause these ventures do not leverage the company's foundation, they involve higher risk and slower profitability. By acknowledg-ing that they are experiments and not part of the core business, companies can establish a budget for experiments, design distinct metrics for assessing the success of each experiment, and allow a realistic amount of time for the most promising experiments to achieve profitability.

4. Use Architecture as a Compass and Communication Tool

Jim Crookes, chief architect at BT, has observed, "Companies get the systems they deserve. A company's systems estate is a result of its culture, organizational history, and its funding structures. Coherent, well-integrated systems will only ever exist in companies that value coherence and integrated service."[12]

Enterprise architecture should guide companies to greater coherence. A one-page core diagram of the enterprise architecture can act as a compass accessed by managers to resolve differences of opinion about next steps in building organizational capabilities. The objective of the enterprise architecture is not so much to achieve a particular end state as it is to serve as a blueprint for the company's direction. It's easy for companies to become enamored with the next big project or new strategic opportunity. But that kind of enthusiasm creates a rush to the next project without ensuring that employees are driving benefits from the last project. Enterprise architecture maps a path in which a company incrementally builds and then leverages capabilities. The company becomes smarter—and more successful.

5. Don't Skip Stages

The architecture maturity stages identify the business transformations necessary to leverage the foundation for execution. Skipping stages leads to either failures or delayed benefits by taking on more organizational change than a company's people can handle. Each stage has very different learning requirements. (See table 4-1). Companies yield huge benefits by driving the value from their current stage. For example, Guardian Life Insurance cut IT costs 30 percent between 2000 and 2003 by consolidating servers, renegotiating contracts, introducing offshore outsourcing, and enforcing financial discipline.[13] That kind of benefit has an immediate impact on the company's bottom line while positioning the company for even more-powerful business benefits.

6. Implement the Foundation One Project at a Time

Some executives are tempted to solve all problems with a single huge effort. Unless a company is on the verge of bankruptcy, however, the big-bang approach is almost never a good idea. Implementing a foundation, one project at a time, uses the momentum of current business needs to create the foundation. In the process, the most important elements of the architecture get implemented first.

Every business has critical strategic initiatives to execute. These initiatives can be implemented quickly with no thought to their long-term impact on the efficiency and flexibility of the business, or they can help implement the foundation for execution. Implementing a foundation one project at a time gives the entire company time to absorb new capabilities and recalibrate its next steps.

7. Don't Do It Alone—Outsource

Defining an operating model, designing an enterprise architecture, and building the foundation for execution are all major undertakings. Every company needs to take control of setting the direction, but it makes sense to get help with the implementation. Over time many of the processes a company standardizes will be candidates for outsourcing. Certainly, some standardized processes will be unique to a company. But whenever world-class providers can find enough customers desiring the same process, companies will have no reason to retain processes internally.

Outsourcing those capabilities that don't distinguish you competitively frees up management attention to focus on activities that will differentiate your company and help you grow profitably. Companies will have to postpone some outsourcing while waiting for an external market to develop, but ultimately, outsourced processes will constitute part of most companies' foundation for execution.

8. Invest in Your People

Automating core activities and providing useful data can release the creativity of the company's people. A foundation for execution presents both an opportunity and a requirement to develop and capitalize on people's capabilities. Most companies woefully underinvest in IT education and training, allocating on average about 2 percent of the typical IT budget to employee development.[14] Worse still, when an economic downturn occurs, training and travel are the first areas to be cut.

Many companies also miss out on the important opportunity for learning that a project postimplementation review offers. Growing numbers of companies now include in their project budgets an allocation for developing people that includes education, training, and postimplementation review. Professional development helps companies generate the expected benefits of new systems—it is also important for motivating and energizing the company's key asset, its people. Postimplementation reviews provide critical feedback into the next round of project justification with data on risk, performance, and resource needs. Leading firms are linking their regular postimplementation reviews to individual performance assessments and incentives.

9. Reward Enterprisewide Thinking

A foundation for execution can be foiled by unaligned incentives. If people are instructed to build and leverage a foundation for execution but rewarded for maximizing local performance, the company's foundation will be disregarded. In recent years State Street moved from a relatively autonomous business unit model to "One State Street." A critical success factor was increasing the sharing and reuse across different business units while still maintaining a culture of innovation.[15] Several factors needed to change. Consequently, a new governance model was implemented, an enterprisewide IT budget was instituted, and more recently, the organization was restructured so that both operations and IT now report to Executive Vice President and CIO Joe Antonellis.

To reinforce the new approach to business, the basis for incentives and bonuses was also changed. Today at State Street, business unit executives typically receive annual incentives based 50 percent on the performance of the business unit and 50 percent on enterprisewide performance, such as earnings per share. All IT professionals—with their responsibility to focus on such company-wide issues as creating a common foundation for execution—receive incentives based 100 percent on enterprisewide performance. This type of bonus structure helps clarify individuals' priorities.

10. Empower Employees with the Foundation for Execution

A foundation for execution is where people, systems, and processes converge to make companies more effective. Some companies, including Verizon Wireless, Lands' End, and Nordstrom, have developed reputations for effective customer interactions. These companies empower their employees to make decisions, provide clear objectives or guidelines for their behavior, and give them powerful systems to guide those decisions. At the end of the workday, employees should find satisfaction in their accomplishments, whether that involves helping customers, designing strategic partnerships, introducing new products, or updating the accounting books. Instead, many employees regularly spend their day reworking tasks that have already been completed, fighting bureaucracy to get approvals for obvious decisions, or manipulating data on tasks that a computer could do faster, better, and cheaper. The promise of the foundation for execution is that a company's people will do more value-added work—and the company will perform far better as a result.

The Journey That Lies Ahead

Enterprise architecture in many companies refers to a detailed blueprint of systems, data, and technology. It is now clear that enterprise architecture is instead a business vision. Enterprise architecture begins at the top—with a statement of how a company operates—and results in a foundation of IT and business process capabilities on which a company builds its competitiveness. Establishing this foundation for execution is a joint responsibility of business and IT executives—it shapes the strategic opportunities a company can respond to in the future. We believe that a number of pressures will make a foundation for execution more important in the coming years.

First, companies will increasingly face customers who demand high service levels at low cost—and competitors will give those customers exactly what they ask for. Market conditions change rapidly—sometimes shaped by customers, sometimes by competitors, but in all cases, requiring a rapid response. Companies without a robust foundation for execution will have a tough time battling competitors who have already automated their process capabilities.

Second, companies will continue to encounter greater technology-related risks and growing regulation. A well-designed foundation simplifies the IT and business environment, thus reducing the risks of systems failures, security and privacy breaches, and loss of data integrity. A simplified IT and business process environment is critical to reducing a company's vulnerability to a wide range of risks. Companies do not have a choice as to whether they want to manage risk—business continuity, security, data integrity, and regulatory compliance must be managed, and managed well.

Third, as we discussed in our prognostications on the fifth stage of architecture maturity, companies will increasingly partner to enter new markets and create new industries. Many of the most exciting strategic opportunities will require companies to quickly join forces—and just as quickly to separate again—exploiting their distinctive competences by linking modular business capabilities. These dynamic partnerships are already becoming important— even though few companies have the technology or business process infrastructure to support them. Companies whose foundation for execution can easily reach across company boundaries and plug and play their modular business capabilities with partners will win in this fast-paced world of global opportunities.

Fourth, vendors will increasingly provide industry-standard business processes for the same or lower cost than companies can provide internally. Increased outsourcing will accelerate the architecture maturity process, so companies will develop more-robust foundations. Companies that have not learned how to implement and manage standardized and integrated processes will struggle with the realities of the marketplace.

A foundation for execution allows a company to automate predictable processes so management can focus on higher-value tasks like innovating, partnering, and identifying new opportunities. The foundation empowers employees and enriches jobs by reducing redundant and tedious tasks while providing the information needed to innovate and customize. Few companies have built a foundation of digitized processes facilitating agility throughout the organization. Those that have are better positioned to take advantage of market opportunities and grow profitably. These leading companies are evidence that the enterprise architecture journey is one worth taking.

Notes

Chapter 1

1. Pete Engardio, Dexter Roberts, and Brian Bremner, "The China Price," *Business Week,* December 6, 2004, Issue 3911.

2. Partha Iyengar, "State of the Information and Communication Technology Industry in India," research report G00126192, Gartner, Stamford, CT, March 28, 2005.

3. To substantiate that these companies were more profitable, we verified that respondents' reported profitability was statistically significantly correlated with the firms' reported three-year financial performance.

4. Our research includes fifty case studies on enterprise architecture and eighteen case studies on the IT engagement model. We conducted two surveys on enterprise architecture that reached 180 companies. In addition, we surveyed 256 companies on IT governance and its influence on architecture.

5. Kei Nagayama and Peter Weill, "7-Eleven Japan Co., Ltd.: Reinventing the Retail Business Model," working paper 338, MIT Sloan Center for Information Systems Research, Cambridge, MA, January 2004.

6. The concept of core capabilities as a source of competitive advantage was developed by a number of researchers. See, for example, Kenneth R. Andrews, *The Concept of Corporate Strategy,* 3rd ed. (Homewood, IL: McGraw Hill/Irwin, 1994) and C. K. Prahalad and Gary Hamel, "The Core Competence of the Corporation," *Harvard Business Review,* May–June 1990, 79–91. Kathleen Eisenhardt refined the concept in her discussion of dynamic capabilities; see, for example, Kathleen M. Eisenhardt and Jeffery A. Martin, "Dynamic Capabilities: What Are They?"

Strategic Management Journal 21, no. 10/11 (2000): 1105–1121. Jay Barney also addressed the concept of core capabilities; see, for example, Jay Barney, "The Resource-Based Theory of the Firm," *Organization Science* 7, no. 5 (1996): 469. We use the concept somewhat differently than these authors: the firm's foundation for execution digitizes not just the capabilities that "make a significant contribution to the perceived customer benefits of the end product" (to use Prahalad and Hamel's view), but also the capabilities that provide the business process integration and standardization necessary for delivering goods and services to customers. Such capabilities may not be "core" in the sense of competitively distinctive, but they are necessary and digitizing these capabilities allows company management to focus on higher-level tasks.

7. As Michael Jordan has shown, however, being great in one arena—basketball—doesn't guarantee success in others, such as golf or baseball. Similarly, a foundation built for one approach to delivering goods and services can limit the ways a company competes.

8. For a discussion of the risks associated with organizational change, see Cyrus Gibson, "IT-Enabled Business Change: An Approach to Understanding and Managing Risk," *MIS Quarterly Executive* 2, no. 2 (September 2003): 105–115.

9. For more details see (1) Sinan Aral and Peter Weill, "IT Assets, Organizational Capabilities, and Firm Performance: Asset and Capability Specific Complementarities," working paper 343, MIT Sloan Center for Information Systems Research, Cambridge, MA, August 2005 and (2) Peter Weill and Sinan Aral, "Generating Premium Returns on Your IT Investments," *MIT Sloan Management Review* 47 no. 2 (Winter 2006): 39–48

10. *The Sarbanes-Oxley Act* of 2002 creates a five-member public-company accounting oversight board, which has the authority to set and enforce auditing, attestation, quality control, and ethics (including independence) standards for auditors of public companies. (From AICPA, "Landmark Accounting Reform Legislation Signed into Law," http://www.aicpa.org/pubs/cpaltr/Sept2002/landmark.htm.) *Basel II* is an effort by international banking supervisors to update the original international bank capital accord (Basel I), which has been in effect since 1988. Current proposals aim to improve the consistency of capital regulations internationally, to make regulatory capital more risk sensitive, and to promote enhanced risk management practices among large, internationally active banking organizations. (From The Federal Reserve Board "Basel II Capital Accord," Federal Reserve Board, http://www.federalreserve.gov/generalinfo/basel2/default.htm.) *The Health Insurance*

Portability and Accountability Act of 1996 (HIPAA) had as a goal "to improve the efficiency and effectiveness of the US health care system by encouraging the widespread use of electronic data interchange in health care." HIPAA established national standards for electronic health-care transactions and addresses the security and privacy of health-care data. (From Centers for Medicare and Medicaid Services, "HIPAA General Information," http://www.cms.hhs.gov/hipaa/.)

11. Enterprise resource planning systems are among the biggest, most complex systems companies can buy. They have multiple modules, encompassing processes such as financial planning and accounting, supply chain management, and human resource management. These systems are known by the vendor's name: SAP, Oracle, and a host of vendors who provide systems for smaller companies.

12. Quotation from video interview with Mike Eskew, chairman and CEO of UPS, with Jeanne Ross and Peter Weill at MIT Sloan School Center for Information Systems Research, Cambridge, MA, April 10, 2002.

13. Both this quotation and the subsequent one from Suzanne Peck are from an interview with Suzanne Peck conducted by Jeanne Ross, May 2005, Washington, DC.

14. Nagayama and Weill, "7-Eleven Japan."

15. Francisco Gonzalez-Meza Hoffmann and Peter Weill, "Banknorth: Designing IT Governance for a Growth-Oriented Business Environment," working paper 350, MIT Sloan Center for Information Systems Research, Cambridge, MA, November 2004.

Chapter 2

1. ThinkExist.com Quotations Online, "Norman Schwarzkopf Quotes," http://en.thinkexist.com/quotes/norman_schwarzkopf/.

2. The measure for strategic effectiveness was a weighted average of the company's priorities for operational efficiency, customer intimacy, product leadership, and strategic agility relative to its success in meeting those objectives.

3. These statistics are based on a survey of 103 companies. These were perceptual measures of how well the company's existing IT-enabled business processes were addressing each of these strategic needs. The first three strategic impacts refer to the disciplines described in Michael Treacy and Fred Wiersema, *The Discipline of Market Leaders: Choose Your Customers, Narrow Your Focus, Dominate Your Market* (Reading, MA: Addison-Wesley, 1995). We have added *strategic agility* because of its growing importance to companies.

4. The description of JM Family Enterprises is from (1) Cynthia M. Beath and Jeanne W. Ross, "JM Family Enterprises, Inc.: Selectively Outsourcing IT for Increased Business Value," MIT Sloan Center for Information Systems Research, forthcoming working paper and (2) Forbes .com, "America's Largest Private Companies," 2005, http://www.forbes .com/finance/lists/21/2004/LIR.jhtml? passListId=21&passYear=2004& passListType=Company&uniqueId=PTGE&datatype=Company.

5. The description of Merrill Lynch is from (1) Merrill Lynch, Annual Report, 2004 and (2) V. Kastori Rangan and Marie Bell, "Merrill Lynch: Integrated Choice," Case 9-500-090 (Boston: Harvard Business School, March 2001).

6. Quoted phrase from V. Kastori Rangan and Marie Bell, "Merrill Lynch: Integrated Choice," Case 9-500-090 (Boston: Harvard Business School, March 2001).

7. Merrill Lynch, Annual Report, 2004.

8. The description of TD Banknorth is extracted from Francisco Gonzalez-Meza Hoffmann and Peter Weill, "Banknorth: Designing IT Governance for a Growth-Oriented Business Environment," working paper 350, MIT Sloan Center for Information Systems Research, Cambridge, MA, November 2004.

9. The description of Dow Chemical is extracted from Jeanne W. Ross and Cynthia M. Beath, "The Federated Broker Model at The Dow Chemical Company: Blending World Class Internal and External Capabilities," working paper 355, MIT Sloan Center for Information Systems Research, Cambridge, MA, July 2005.

10. See Jeanne W. Ross, "Johnson & Johnson: Building an Infrastructure to Support Global Operations," working paper 283, MIT Sloan Center for Information Systems Research, Cambridge, MA, September 1995.

11. Clayton M. Christensen, *The Innovator's Dilemma: When New Technologies Cause Great Firms to Fail* (Boston: Harvard Business School Press, 1997).

12. The example company's industry has been disguised, but it has many characteristics of the packaging industry.

13. The Schneider National vignette is drawn from Jeanne W. Ross, "Schneider National Inc.: Building Networks to Add Customer Value," working paper 285, MIT Sloan Center for Information Systems Research, Cambridge, MA, September 1995.

Chapter 3

1. Troy Taylor, "The Winchester Mystery House: The History of One of America's Most Haunted Houses," "Ghosts of the Prairie, America's

Most Haunted Places," 2001, http://www.prairieghosts.com/winchester
.html.

2. Richard Woodham and Peter Weill, "Manheim Interactive: Selling Cars Online," working paper 314, MIT Sloan Center for Information Systems Research, Cambridge, MA, February 2001.

3. Nils O. Fonstad and David C. Robertson, "Realizing IT-Enabled
Change: The IT Engagement Model," research briefing IV, no. 3D, MIT
Sloan Center for Information Systems Research, Cambridge, MA, Octo-
ber 2005.

4. The Delta Air Lines vignette is drawn from Jeanne W. Ross,
"E-business at Delta Air Lines: Extracting Value from a Multi-Faceted Ap-
proach," working paper 317, MIT Sloan Center for Information Systems
Research, Cambridge, MA, August 2001. See also "E-business at Delta Air
Lines: Extracting Value from a Multi-Faceted Approach," Video Case
317-V, MIT Sloan Center for Information Systems Research, August 2001.

5. The Carlson vignette is drawn from Nils O. Fonstad and Jeanne
W. Ross, "Case Vignette of Carlson," (Cambridge, MA: MIT Sloan School
of Management Center for Information Systems Research, January 2003).

6. Individual business units in diversification companies like Carlson often have separate core diagrams reflecting greater standardization and integration (and thus a different operating model).

7. This case is derived from Peter Weill and Jeanne W. Ross, *IT Governance: How Top Performers Manage IT Decision Rights for Superior Results*
(Boston: Harvard Business School Press, 2004), 27–34.

8. The ING DIRECT vignette is drawn from David C. Robertson,
"ING Direct: The IT Challenge (B)," working paper IMD-3-1345, IMD,
Lausanne, Switzerland, 2003, 5.

9. Martin Vonk, "ING DIRECT: ICT and Governance" (presentation at IMD, Lausanne, Switzerland, June 29, 2005).

Chapter 4

1. See project information on the Big Dig at http://www.massturn
pike.com/bigdig/background/index.html.

2. Associated Press, "Boston's Big Dig Opens to Public," MSNBC
.com, December 20, 2003, http://msnbc.msn.com/id/3769829/.

3. The concept of architecture stages was introduced in Jeanne W.
Ross, "Creating a Strategic Architecture Competency: Learning in Stages,"
MIS Quarterly Executive 2, no. 1 (March 2003): 31–43.

4. See Jeanne W. Ross, "Maturity Matters: How Firms Generate Value
from Enterprise Architecture," research briefing IV, no. 2B, MIT Sloan
Center for Information Systems Research, Cambridge, MA, July 2004.

5. For a description of the potential of Web services, see John Hagel and John Seely Brown, "Your Next IT Strategy," *Harvard Business Review,* October 2001, 105–113.

6. Jim McGrane, interview by Jeanne W. Ross, September 2002. See Peter Weill and Jeanne W. Ross, *IT Governance: How Top Performers Manage IT Decision Rights for Superior Results* (Boston: Harvard Business School Press, 2004).

7. See Wesley M. Cohen and Daniel A. Levinthal, "Absorptive Capacity: A New Perspective on Learning and Innovation," *Administrative Science Quarterly* 35, no.1 (March 1990): 128–152.

8. Geoffrey E. Bock, "The Guardian Life Insurance Company of America: Improving Business Responsiveness with an Extensive Enterprise Infrastructure," IBM, http://www-306.ibm.com/software/success /cssdb.nsf/CS/BEMY-5UH33J?OpenDocument&Site=software, December 2003.

9. Air Products and Chemicals, Annual Report, 2004.

10. Respondents rated their profitability relative to competitors on a scale of 1 to 5. These ratings were significantly correlated to a three-year average return on invested capital.

Chapter 5

1. Paul A. David, "The Dynamo and the Computer: An Historical Perspective on the Modern Productivity Paradox," *American Economic Review* 80, no. 2 (May 1990).

2. Andrew Hagadorn, *How Breakthroughs Happen* (Boston: Harvard Business School Press, 2003), 36–46.

3. George Westerman and Robert Walpole, "PFPC: Building an IT Risk Management Competency," working paper 352, MIT Sloan Center for Information Systems Research, Cambridge, MA, April 2005.

4. For this analysis we used stage 1 budgets as a baseline for IT budgets and compared it to the IT budgets of companies in other stages, controlling for industry differences.

5. Karl Wachs, interview by Peter Weill, George Westerman, and Nils O. Fonstad, videotape recording, Cambridge, MA, May 5, 2005.

6. Charlie Feld, interview by Jeanne W. Ross, videotape recording, Cambridge, MA, April 15, 2002.

7. Westerman and Walpole, "PFPC."

8. Jim Barrington, interview by Peter Weill, George Westerman, and Nils O. Fonstad, videotape recording, March 25, 2005.

9. The first three strategic impacts refer to the disciplines described in Michael Treacy and Fred Wiersema, *The Discipline of Market Leaders:*

Choose Your Customers, Narrow Your Focus, Dominate Your Market (Reading, MA: Addison-Wesley, 1995). We have added *strategic agility* because of its growing importance to companies.

10. Jeanne W. Ross, "Dow Corning Corporation: Case Studies A, B, and C," working paper 305, MIT Sloan Center for Information Systems Research, Cambridge, MA, June 1999.

11. Rebecca Rhoads, "RTN on Governance" (presentation at the MIT Sloan Center for Information Systems Research Summer Session, June 2005).

12. Ibid.

13. Al-Noor Ramji, interview by George Westerman and Nils O. Fonstad, videotape recording, Cambridge, MA, May 19, 2005.

14. Ibid.

15. The description of Schindler's stages, and the corresponding quotations, are from Brent Glendening, interview by David C. Robertson, Ebikon, Switzerland, May 2003.

Chapter 6

1. Daniel Robey, Jeanne W. Ross, and Marie-Claude Boudreau, "Learning to Implement Enterprise Systems: An Exploratory Study of the Dialectics of Change," *Journal of Management Information Systems* 19, no. 1 (Summer 2002): 17–45.

2. The term *IT engagement model* was introduced by Nils O. Fonstad and David C. Robertson. See Fonstad and Robertson, "Realizing IT-Enabled Change: The IT Engagement Model," research briefing IV, no. 3D, MIT Sloan Center for Information Systems Research, Cambridge, MA, October 2005. For more on the IT engagement model, Fonstad and Robertson, "Transforming a Company Project by Project: The IT Engagement Model," *MIS Quarterly Executive* 5, no. 1 (March 2006).

3. This section draws on Peter Weill and Jeanne W. Ross, "A Matrixed Approach to Designing IT Governance," *MIT Sloan Management Review* 46, no. 2 (Winter 2005): 26–34.

4. The information on UNICEF is drawn from Peter Weill and Jeanne W. Ross, *IT Governance: How Top Performers Manage IT Decision Rights for Superior Results* (Boston: Harvard Business School Press, 2004), pp. 206–210.

5. Ibid., 210.

6. Ibid.

7. Ibid.

8. Information systems textbooks provide an introductory view of alternative project life cycles. For example, Steven Alter describes

four phases; E. Wainwright Martin and his coauthors list three phases encompassing eight steps; Efraim Turban, Ephraim McLean, and James Wetherbe list eight stages; Kenneth C. Laudon and Jane P. Laudon describe six steps with fourteen activities. See Alter, *Information Systems: Foundation of E-business,* 4th ed. (Upper Saddle River, NJ: Prentice Hall, 2002); Martin et al., *Managing Information Technology,* 4th ed. (Upper Saddle River, NJ: Prentice Hall, 2002); Laudon and Laudon, *Management Information Systems: Managing the Digital Firm,* 9th ed. (Upper Saddle River, NJ: Pearson Prentice Hall, 2006); Turban, McLean, and Wetherbe, *Information Technology for Management: Transforming Organizations in the Digital Economy,* 4th ed. (New York: Wiley, 2004).

9. All quoted material relating to Raytheon drawn from Rebecca Rhoads, "RTN on Governance" (presentation at the MIT Sloan Center for Information Systems Research Summer Session, June 2005).

10. This section draws from Peter Heinckiens interview by David C. Robertson, Lausanne, Switzerland, July 2005.

11. Ludo Vandervelden, interview by Peter M. Heinckiens, Brussels, July 2005.

12. In the Toyota production system every employee has the right and duty to stop the line if a quality problem occurs.

13. Toyota Motor Marketing Europe's architecture and how it is measured is based on Peter M. Heinckiens, "Meta-Level Business Integration for Supporting New-Economy Business Models" (PhD diss., University of Ghent, May 2004).

14. This example has been disguised at the company's request. Dates and names of committees have been changed, but the structure of committees and performance results are accurate.

15. Jim Crookes, interview by Nils O. Fonstad and David C. Robertson, London, March 2004.

Chapter 7

1. Dan Ikenson, "Ending the Chicken War," trade briefing paper 17, Cato Institute, Washington, DC, June 2003.

2. See www.forrester.com and www.gartner.com for reports on the outcomes of outsourcing.

3. For an example of an HR partnership, see Mary C. Lacity, David Feeny, and Leslie P. Willcocks, "Transforming a Back-Office Function: Lessons from BAE Systems' Experience with an Enterprise Partnership," *MIS Quarterly Executive* 2, no. 2 (September 2003): 86–103.

4. While there is much debate as to what constitutes a *core compe-*

tency, the belief that core competencies should not be outsourced has gained considerable traction. See, for example, James Bryant Quinn, "Strategic Outsourcing: Leveraging Knowledge Capabilities," *Sloan Management Review* 40, no. 4 (1999): 9–21.

5. This case study is adapted from Cynthia M. Beath and Jeanne W. Ross, "Campbell Soup Company: Creating Business Value Through an IT Partnership," working paper, MIT Sloan Center for Information Systems Research, forthcoming. Additional quotations are from an interview with Doreen Wright by Cynthia M. Beath and Jeanne W. Ross, February 9, 2005, Camden, New Jersey.

6. The concept of IS Lite was developed by Gartner. See Chuck Tucker and Roger Woolfe, "The Reality of IS Lite," Gartner EXP Premier Report, September 2003.

7. Katie M. Kaiser and Stephen Hawk, "Evolution of Offshore Software Development: From Outsourcing to Cosourcing," *MIS Quarterly Executive* 3, no. 2 (June 2004): 69–81.

8. Third-party expertise was identified as a critical success factor in ERP implementations in Carol Brown and Iris Vessey, "Managing the Next Wave of Enterprise Systems: Leveraging Lessons from ERP," *MIS Quarterly Executive* 2, no. 1 (March 2003): 65–77.

9. This case study is adapted from (1) Henri Bourgeois and David C. Robertson, "Liverpool City Council (A): The ICT Outsourcing Decision," Case IMD-3-1289 (Lausanne, Switzerland: IMD, 2004) and (2) Henri Bourgeois and David C. Robertson, "Liverpool City Council (B): Co-sourcing Public Services Through a Joint Venture with BT," Case IMD-3-1290 (Lausanne, Switzerland: IMD, 2004).

10. This case study is adapted from Jeanne W. Ross and Cynthia M. Beath, "The Federated Broker Model at The Dow Chemical Company: Blending World Class Internal and External Capabilities," working paper 355, MIT Sloan Center for Information Systems Research, Cambridge, MA, July 2005.

11. Andrew Liveris, "Letter to the Stockholders of The Dow Chemical Company," February 9, 2005.

12. Both this quotation and the subsequent two are from Ross and Beath, "Federated Broker Model."

Chapter 8

1. For more on platform development, see David Robertson and Karl Ulrich "Planning for Product Platforms," *Sloan Management Review* 39, no. 4, Summer 1998: 19–31.

2. Parts of this case are drawn from (1) Jeanne W. Ross et al., "United Parcel Service: Business Transformation Through Information Technology," working paper 331, MIT Sloan Center for Information Systems Research, Cambridge, MA, September 2002; (2) Jeanne W. Ross, "United Parcel Service: Delivering Packages and E-Commerce Solutions," working paper 318, MIT Sloan Center for Information Systems Research, Cambridge, MA, August 2001; (3) Mike Eskew, interview by Peter Weill and Jeanne W. Ross, videotape recording, Cambridge, MA, April 10, 2002.

3. Parts of this case are drawn from (1) Kei Nagayama and Peter Weill, "7-Eleven Japan Co., Ltd.: Reinventing the Retail Business Model," working paper 338, MIT Sloan Center for Information Systems Research, Cambridge, MA, January 2004; (2) Peter Weill and Michael R. Vitale, *Place to Space: Migrating to eBusiness Models* (Boston: Harvard Business School Press, 2001); (3) Ben M. Bensaou "Seven-Eleven Japan: Managing a Networked Organization," case study 05/7-4690, INSEAD Euro-Asia Centre, May 1997;(4) Seven-Eleven Japan, "Corporate Outline 2004," http://www.sej.co.jp/english/investor/irtool/co2004_e.html.

4. Bensaou "Seven-Eleven Japan."

5. While SEJ's standardized systems give headquarters a great deal of transparency about inventory levels, supply chain operations, and sales, we don't classify the company as a Unification operating model because data flows to corporate, not to other business units. In other words, business unit activities do not depend on receiving data from other business units.

6. Bensaou, "Seven-Eleven Japan."

7. This case is derived from Steven Sheinheit, "Evolution of IT Architecture at MetLife" (presentation at the MIT Sloan Center for Information Systems Research Summer Session, June 2005) and from MetLife, Annual Report, 2004 (available at http://library.corporate-ir.net/library/12/121/121171/items/142153/MET_2004AR.pdf).

8. This case is drawn from (1) Rebecca Chung, Donald Marchand, and William Kettinger, "The CEMEX Way: The Right Balance Between Local Business Flexibility and Global Standardization," Case IMD-3-1341 (Lausanne, Switzerland: IMD, 2005) and (2) Rebecca Chung, Katarina Paddack, and Donald Marchand, "CEMEX: Global Growth Through Superior Information Capabilities," Case IMD-3-0953 (Lausanne, Switzerland: IMD, 2003).

9. Chung, Paddack, and Marchand, "CEMEX: Global Growth," 5.

10. Chung, Marchand, and Kettinger, "CEMEX Way," 1.

11. Normally, executives refer to the process of developing synergies with an acquisition as "integration." However, because we are using the term differently, we have chosen to refer to CEMEX's approach to acquisitions as "assimilation"—bringing the companies onto standard processes, but not integrating processes across business units.

12. Chung, Paddack, and Marchand, "CEMEX: Global Growth," 7.

13. Eskew, interview by Weill and Ross.

14. Ross et al., "United Parcel Service: Business Transformation."

15. Bensaou, "Seven-Eleven Japan."

16. "Brainy Quote," 2005, http://www.brainyquote.com/quotes /quotes/t/thomasjeff129997.html.

17. The section on Dow Chemical, including the accompanying quotation from Dave Kepler, is based on Jeanne W. Ross and Cynthia M. Beath, "The Federated Broker Model at The Dow Chemical Company: Blending World Class Internal and External Capabilities," working paper 355, MIT Sloan Center for Information Systems Research, Cambridge, MA, July 2005.

Chapter 9

1. "Brainy Quote," 2005, http://www.brainyquote.com/quotes/au thors/f/frank_a_clark.html.

2. Gary Beach, "Repeal Sarbanes-Oxley," *CIO Magazine*, April 1, 2005.

3. A survey of 649 companies by Gartner Worldwide Benchmarking Survey, 2005, found that the more efficient public companies spent less than 4% of their overall 2005 IT budget on regulatory compliance. Source: Dr. Howard Rubin.

4. Peter Weill and Sinan Aral, "IT Savvy Pays Off: How Top Performers Match IT Portfolios and Organizational Practices," working paper 353, MIT Sloan Center for Information Systems Research, Cambridge, MA, May 2005.

5. This information comes from an MIT Sloan Center for Information Systems Research study of 147 companies' IT investment and performance from 1998 to 2002. For more details see (1) Sinan Aral and Peter Weill, "IT Assets, Organizational Capabilities, and Firm Performance: Asset and Capability Specific Complementarities," working paper 343, MIT Sloan Center for Information Systems Research, Cambridge, MA, August 2005; and (2) Peter Weill and Sinan Aral, "Generating Premium Returns on Your IT Investments," MIT *Sloan Management Review* 47, no. 2 (Winter 2006): 39–48.

6. Stephanie Overby, "The Price Is Always Right," *CIO Magazine*, February 15, 2005.

7. See Hewlett-Packard, "Infrastructure Management 2005,"http:// h41137.www4.hp.com/tpm/uk/en/ppuservices/infrastructure-man-agement.html.

8. See note 5.

9. Peter Weill and Jeanne W. Ross, *IT Governance: How Top Performers Manage IT Decision Rights for Superior Results* (Boston: Harvard Business School Press, 2004).

10. Many of the examples in this section are further descriptions or summaries of examples in earlier chapters where the sources are identified.

11. Kenneth R. Andrews, *The Concept of Corporate Strategy,* 3d ed. (Homewood, IL: McGraw Hill/Irwin, 1994); C. K. Prahalad and Gary Hamel, "The Core Competence of the Corporation," *Harvard Business Review,* May–June 1990, 79–91; Kathleen M. Eisenhardt and Jeffery A. Martin, "Dynamic Capabilities: What Are They?" *Strategic Management Journal* 21, no. 10/11 (2000): 1105–1121; and Jay Barney, "The Resource-Based Theory of the Firm," *Organization Science* 7, no. 5 (1996): 469.

12. Jim Crookes's e-mail message to Jeanne Ross, November 2005.

13. Dennis Callahan and Rick Omartian, "A New Breed of IT Exec," *FinanceTech,* February 4, 2004, http://www.financetech.com/featured /showArticle.jhtml?articleID=17602496.

14. Dr. Howard Rubin, Gartner Worldwide Benchmarking Survey, 2005.

15. Peter Weill and Richard Woodham, "State Street Corporation: Evolving IT Governance," working paper 327, MIT Sloan Center for Information Systems Research, Cambridge, MA, August 2002.

Index

About the Authors

Jeanne W. Ross is Principal Research Scientist at the MIT Sloan School's Center for Information Systems Research (CISR). CISR undertakes practical empirical research on how firms generate business value from IT and is funded by corporate patrons and sponsors. The center disseminates its findings through briefings, papers, workshops, and executive education. At MIT Jeanne lectures, conducts research, and teaches public and customized executive courses on IT management. She has published widely, including journal articles, book chapters, and case studies. Her prior book, *IT Governance: How Top Performers Manage IT Decision Rights for Superior Results,* coauthored with Peter Weill, was published by Harvard Business School Press in 2004. Jeanne's research focuses on how businesses generate value from IT. She regularly speaks at major forums, discussing IT management and value. As Editor in Chief of *MIS Quarterly Executive,* she is working to increase collaboration between the academic and professional IT communities.

Peter Weill is Director of the MIT Sloan School's Center for Information Systems Research and an MIT Senior Research Scientist. His research and advisory work centers on the strategic impact, value, and governance of IT in enterprises. He has presented widely at industry forums, executive education, and MBA programs on the business value of IT and has published award-winning books, journal articles, and case studies. These include his book with Jeanne W. Ross, *IT Governance.* He also coauthored the bestselling *Leveraging the New Infrastructure: How Market Leaders Capitalize on Information Technology* (Harvard Business

School Press, 1998) and *Place to Space: Migrating to eBusiness Models* (Harvard Business School Press, 2001), which won one of the *Library Journal of America*'s best business book of the year awards. Peter is currently researching business agility and which business models will be most successful.

David C. Robertson is a professor at IMD in Lausanne, Switzerland, where he teaches innovation, technology management, and IT in the school's executive and MBA programs. At IMD, David is currently directing executive programs for Credit Suisse, EMC, Skanska, and HSBC. He was also codirector of Making Business Sense of IT, a joint program between IMD and MIT. Prior to IMD, David was a postdoctoral research fellow at the MIT Computer Science and Artificial Intelligence Laboratory, a consultant at McKinsey & Co., and an executive at four enterprise software companies. In addition to his responsibilities at IMD, David is cofounder of a product design firm that is patenting and bringing its first product to market, and he serves as a consultant to companies on such issues as innovation, enterprise architecture, and overall business strategy.